Run for your Life!

Run for Your Life!

THE COMPLETE MARATHON GUIDE

DR BEN TAN

Marshall Cavendish Editions

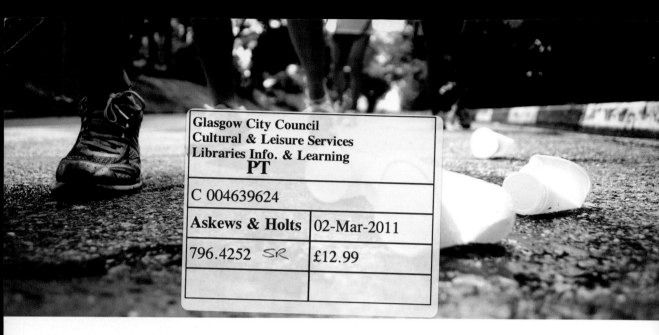

Cover image: Elements by the Box
Contributors' page: All images by Elements by the Box except 7,8,10,16,19 (contributors' own) • Courtesy of Dr. Ben Tan: 5, 33, 83–84, 129, 134, 136, 137 (right), 138, 140 (bottom left & right), 141, 142, 143, 158 • Courtesy of Singapore Footcare Centre: 186 (top left & right), 191 • Illustrations by Anuar bin Abdul Rahim: 39, 43, 85, 86, 98, 135 (right), 140 (top), 146, 159, 161, 186 • © Leslie Tan/REDSPORTS. SG: 29 • Renaissance Pictures: 137 (bottom left), 135 (left) • All other images by Elements by the Box
Models: Adele Ang, Chee Wai Siong, Benny Goh, Malia Ho, Daniel Ling, and Ben Tan

Design concept and art direction: Lock Hong Liang

Published by Marshall Cavendish Editions
An imprint of Marshall Cavendish International
1 New Industrial Road, Singapore 536196

Other Marshall Cavendish Offices
Marshall Cavendish Ltd. 5th Floor 32–38 Saffron Hill, London EC1N 8FH • Marshall Cavendish Corporation. 99 White Plains Road, Tarrytown NY 10591-9001, USA • Marshall Cavendish International (Thailand) Co Ltd. 253 Asoke, 12th Flr, Sukhumvit 21 Road, Klongtoey Nua, Wattana, Bangkok 10110, Thailand • Marshall Cavendish (Malaysia) Sdn Bhd, Times Subang, Lot 46, Subang Hi-Tech Industrial Park, Batu Tiga, 40000 Shah Alam, Selangor Darul Ehsan, Malaysia

Marshall Cavendish is a trademark of Times Publishing Limited

National Library Board Singapore Cataloguing in Publication Data
Tan, Ben.
Run for your life! : the complete marathon guide/Ben Tan. – Singapore : Marshall Cavendish Editions, 2009.
p. cm.
ISBN-13 : 978-981-261-781-1 (pbk.)

1. Marathon running. 2. Marathon running – Training. I. Title.

GV1065
796.4252 — dc22   OCN433413478

Printed in Singapore by Fabulous Printers

To the growing running community in Singapore, including my regular training partners who kept me company and encouraged me on my long runs, and pushed me during intensive workouts.

To my 13-year-old German Shepherd, Draco, who paced me on my 12 km runs during his hey days.

And last but not least, to my lovely wife, Alison, who once believed that completing 2.4 km would kill her, and now regularly participates in local and overseas distance races together with me.

Ben and Alison at the Prague International Marathon 2004

Contents

Foreword

September 2008, Berlin. Daniel Ling (2007 Singapore Marathon champion) and I had just completed the Berlin Marathon earlier in the day. Dr Ben Tan ran in the same marathon, finishing the race in 3:01:15. Certainly impressive for a 40-year-old medical doctor and former sailor, with no background in track and field. To top it off, he had dengue fever only a month earlier!

As a running coach, I thought it was a matter of time before he went under three hours. Almost all the Singaporeans who took part in the Berlin Marathon arranged to have dinner that evening, and that was when I first got to know Ben. It was then that I invited him to train with Daniel and I, with the aim of going sub-3 at the Singapore Marathon just two months away. Being the athlete that he is, Ben accepted my challenge, and started training.

Despite his busy work schedule, he joined Daniel, my Hwa Chong Institution runners, and I each Saturday evening for workouts. On the other days, he trained on his own or with his regular training partners. Ben's determination, systematic approach, and focus were evident during training. I could see why he is an Asian Games and four-time Southeast Asian Games gold medallist in sailing, and three-time Sportsman of the Year. He understood and absorbed training concepts easily. He could process information, adapting and customising it to his needs. So it was no surprise that Ben comfortably ran a sub-3 (2:56:20) at the 2008 Singapore Marathon, even though it was much hotter than in Berlin!

I've dedicated my life to running, and it is worth every minute that I spend on it. The desire to reach one's potential, hard work and know-how are the necessary ingredients. Nothing beats the feeling of completing your first full marathon, or knowing that you've given it your best. I know Ben understands this, and that is why he has chosen to share his journey towards a sub-3 with others through this book.

Dr Ben Tan is a sports physician, and he makes full use of this sports medicine and sports science training to squeeze every ounce of performance from his body. His systematic and holistic approach will certainly help other runners fast track their progress towards their personal goals. Ever the team player, Ben has also roped in the best experts Singapore can offer in various aspects of running — the collective knowledge base makes this book highly comprehensive, balanced, and holistic.

Whether you are a 3- or 6-hour marathoner, I personally feel you can make a breakthrough and significantly improve your time by applying the methods from this detailed and meaningful book. Along the way, you will also find yourself setting personal best times for your 2.4 km, 5 km, 10 km, 15 km, and half marathon times as well!

With this book, you too can bask in the glory of achieving your personal best!

Murugiah Rameshon
National record holder for the marathon (2:24)
Winner, Singapore Marathon, 2008

Dr Ben Tan started his sporting career as a sailor at the age of 11 and went on to become an Olympian (1996), Asian Games Gold medallist (1994, Hiroshima), and four-time consecutive Southeast Asian Games Gold medallist (1989, 1991, 1993, 1995). His first book, *The Complete Introduction to Laser Racing*, was hailed by *Yachts and Yachting* magazine as the "Best Laser Racing book ever!" Considered the "Bible" for Laser sailors worldwide, the book has been translated into Chinese, Japanese, and Polish. Singapore's three-time Sportsman of the Year (1991, 1994, 1995) retired from sailing in 1996.

Dr Tan took up distance running only towards the end of 2002, finishing his first marathon in 5 hours 35 minutes. Morphing from a 78-kg strength athlete that is requisite of a Laser sailor, to a lean 63-kg distance runner, Dr Tan not only achieved his aim of completing the marathon in less than three hours (2:56:20) at the 2008 Singapore Marathon, but also had a podium finish. En route, he qualified for and competed in the 2007 Boston Marathon (3:19:04), 2008 Berlin Marathon (3:01:15), and 10 other marathons.

Dr Ben Tan graduated with an MBBS in 1991 and obtained his masters in sports medicine from the Australian Institute of Sport and University of Canberra in 1997. As deputy director at the Sports Medicine & Research Centre (Singapore Sports Council), Dr Tan expanded the Sports Council's Sports Science services to the benefit of our national athletes. The pioneering doctor then chaired a workgroup that established sports medicine as a medical subspecialty in Singapore. Currently, Dr Tan is the head & senior consultant sports physician at the Changi Sports Medicine Centre (CSMC) and concurrently the medical director of the Singapore Sports Medicine Centre. He is a published author in peer-reviewed sports medicine and sports science journals.

In 2003, Dr Tan chaired SingaporeSailing's High Peformance Sailing Committee that installed the training and competition framework that has produced Singapore's World titles (14 to date in sailing). In 2007, Dr Tan chaired the Sports Safety Committee that established Singapore's current national sports safety guidelines. Dr Tan is also the vice-chairman of the medical commission of the International Sailing Federation, deputy president of SingaporeSailing, the vice-chairman of the medical committee of the Football Association of Singapore, member of the Singapore Sports Council and the Singapore National Olympic Council (SNOC), chairman of the SNOC Athletes' Commission, and the sports patron of the Singapore Disability Sports Council. His contributions to sports have earned him a Public Service Medal (1993), Public Service Star (1995), the Singapore Youth Award (1995), and Singapore Youth Award Medal of Commendation (2004).

01" **Adele Ang** is a senior physiotherapist at the Singapore Sports Medicine Centre. She graduated from the School of Physiotherapy at Curtin University, Perth, Western Australia in 1995 and proceeded to do a Master of Physiotherapy (Musculoskeletal) in the year 2000 after five years of clinical experience. She obtained most of her clinical experience by working closely with sports physicians in the treatment of sports injuries amongst national athletes in the Singapore Sports Council. She has over 12 years of clinical experience as well as teaching experience for sports and musculoskeletal physiotherapy, having also taught in the diploma course for physiotherapy at Nanyang Polytechnic in Singapore. Adele believes in constantly upgrading her professional skills and always tries to apply her knowledge to benefit her patients' progress and recovery. She is currently furthering her knowledge in using the pilates system in rehabilitating sports injuries and improving sports performance, especially amongst runners and other endurance sports. She believes that core training using the pilates system can improve both sports performance and reduce the recurrence and occurrence of overuse injuries of the spine and peripheral joints, such as the knees and shoulders.

02" **Shamsynar Ani** is a senior sports physiotherapist at the Changi Sports Medicine Centre and the Singapore Sports Medicine Centre. Her clientele includes elite, recreational and aspiring athletes.

Shamsynar graduated in 2000 from King's College, London (UK), with a masters in science in physiotherapy, having received the Overseas Specialist Awards (Paramedical) scholarship. She was further awarded the Overseas Masters Programme by Changi General Hospital and obtained a masters in musculoskeletal and sports physiotherapy from University of South Australia (Australia) in 2006.

She is currently developing a protocol in the assessment and treatment of knee injuries, particularly in runners and triathletes. Her other areas of interests include rehabilitation of shoulder injuries, health issues that affect youth in sports and netball.

03" **Dr Jason Chia** graduated from the National University of Singapore (1998) and obtained his post-graduate specialist degree, masters of sports medicine from Australia (2002). He is a consultant sports physician in the Changi Sports Medicine Centre and the Singapore Sports Medicine Centre, where he is involved with sports injury management, fitness testing and exercise prescription, weight management, extra corporeal shockwave therapy (ESWT) as well as gait analysis. He oversees the exercise testing service in the Changi Sports Medicine Centre. Dr Chia was involved in the publication of the book, *Prescribing Exercise: A Handbook for Medical Practitioners* and conducts research in ESWT and biomechanics. He is a past president of the Sports Medicine Association of Singapore (2006 – 2007).

Dr Chia previously served as the team physician for Singapore's contingents in the Asian and Southeast Asian Games. In addition, he has been the medical director for sporting events including the OSIM triathlon (2005 – 2008), the Aviva Ironman (2007) and the HSBC Wakeboarding Championship (2005 – 2007).

Dr Chia's interest is in multi-discipline endurance sports. He has completed an Ironman triathlon and now runs marathons recreationally.

04" **Dr William Chin** graduated with an MBBS from Sydney, one of the sporting capitals of the world. He is currently a medical officer with the Changi General Hospital Sports Medicine Centre in Singapore. As an ex-competitive cross-country and track runner during his varsity days, he has discovered a new passion in endurance events like marathons, ironman and adventure races in recent years. His main aim for the year is to achieve a personal best timing in the Singapore Marathon. Occasionally, he dreams of qualifying for the Kona Ironman World Championship in Hawaii.

05" **Elangovan S/O Ganesan** represented Singapore in middle and long distance running at events such as the Asian Track & Field Meet, World Championships in Seville, Spain, and Southeast Asian Games. He won the Singapore Marathon (men's closed category) consecutively from 2004 to 2006, and has a personal best of 2:45:03. He is also a seven-time Singapore national cross-country open champion, nine-time Sheare's Bridge men's closed champion (personal best 1:09:44), two-time Real Run 10 km men's open champion (2005, 2006), and winner of the Johor-Singapore Second Link 10 km men's open (2006). His other personal bests include: 3,000 m in 8min 48.8 sec (All-Comers Meet 1996 Singapore), 1,500 m in 3 min 58.3 sec (Taiwan open 1998), 3,000 m steeplechase in 9 min 18.0 sec (Thailand open 1999), 5,000 m in 15 min 06.6 sec (Berlin open, Germany 2001), and 10,000 m in 31 min 22.0s (Cottbus, Germany 2001).

Coach Elangovan obtained his diploma in sports and exercise sciences in 2005 from Blackburn College, is a certified coach registered with the National Registry of Coaches, and is on the Singapore Athletic Association's panel of coaches for middle and long distance running. He received the Singapore Sports Council's Coach Recognition Award from 2004 to 2006.

Elangovan is presently coaching St Joseph's Institution's distance running team, Pei Hwa Presbyterian and Balestier Hill Primary's track and field teams.

06″ Malia Ho was awarded the Public Service Commission Scholarship to study podiatry in the University of Salford (UK), where she graduated with an honours degree in 1998. She also received sponsorship to pursue her postgraduate degree and graduated from National University of Singapore with a masters in science (by research) in 2002.

She worked at Tan Tock Seng Hospital and NHG polyclinics before setting up Singapore Footcare Centre — the private arm of the Podiatry Service in the National Healthcare Group. As principal podiatrist, she led a team of fellow podiatrists, nurses and assistants in increasing the awareness of podiatry and good foot care to the general public. Malia is now a sports podiatrist at the Singapore Sports Medicine Centre where she manages an array of sports injuries and biomechanical problems of the lower limb.

Malia is an active member of the Podiatry Association and is also a member of the Society of Chiropodists and Podiatrists (UK). She also lectures at various polytechnics and institutions. Her area of interest is in the biomechanics of the lower limb.

07″ Adam Jorgensen completed his podiatry degree with distinction at the Queensland University of Technology, Brisbane, Australia. Following practice in high-risk diabetic foot centres in Brisbane, Adam came to Singapore in 1995 to establish the podiatry service at the National University Hospital. As one of the pioneers of podiatry in Singapore, Adam was also a founding member of the Podiatry Association (Singapore) and is currently its president.

Since 2000, Adam has focused his podiatry interests in sports podiatry. He has had a wealth of experience in the areas of biomechanics, foot running injuries and running shoes. Adam is a member of the Australian Academy of Podiatric Sports Medicine. He has also maintained a close relationship with the Sports Medicine Association (Singapore) having served terms as an executive committee member as well as a term as president in 2006. He has been called upon once again in 2009 as the association president.

In 2004, Adam moved into private practice to establish The Foot Practice at Camden Medical Centre. The Foot Practice continues to expand with new centres at the Singapore Sports Medicine Centre in Novena Medical Centre and Body with Soul at Rochester Park established in 2008.

08" **Sharon Khoo** graduated with a diploma in remedial massage and diploma of sports and athletic support services, from Australasian College of Natural Therapies in Sydney in 2005. Upon graduating she worked as a sports massage therapist at Singapore Sports Council, catering to the national athletes. She is currently a sports massage therapist at the Singapore Sports Medicine Centre. Sharon is also a registered nurse, enabling her to adopt a clinical approach to sports massage.

09" **Darek Lam** is a senior sports physiotherapist at the Changi Sports Medicine Centre and the Singapore Sports Medicine Centre. He manages both elite and recreational athletes.

In 2000, Darek received the prestigious Overseas Specialist Awards (Paramedical) scholarship and he graduated with bachelor of science (Hons) in physiotherapy from the University of Manchester (UK) in 2003. He was later also awarded the Overseas Masters Programme by Changi General Hospital and went on to obtain a masters in sports physiotherapy at the University of Queensland (Australia) in 2007.

He has a special interest in the treatment of knee injuries in runners. He is also actively involved in the research of patello-femoral pain syndrome and has presented in international conferences.

10" **Dr Darren Leong** is a medical officer at Changi Sports Medicine Centre. He graduated with a medical degree from the National University of Singapore in 2005 and is currently pursing a masters in sports medicine.

Darren is an avid tennis player; and having picked up tennis since he was 9, he has represented his schools, (Raffles Institution, Raffles Junior College and the National University of Singapore), and the Singapore Armed Forces (SAF Sports Association) in tennis competitions through the years. While traditionally adept at racket and ball sports, Darren has recently taken a greater interest in other sports such as running, swimming and wakeboarding. He has not completed a full marathon yet, but has been inspired by the story of Phidippides to pursue this goal.

11" **Dr Lim Baoying** graduated with an MBBS from the National University of Singapore in 2006. Currently a medical officer in government service, her interests are in sports medicine and orthopaedic surgery, especially the former where she enjoys working with athletes. She is working towards obtaining a masters of medicine (family medicine) and then proceeding to sports medicine traineeship thereafter.

An athlete herself since junior college days when she was a school representative in national track and field and cross-country meets, she moved on to her first marathon in 1999 at the end of her first year in junior college. She stopped running completely for four years from 2004 – 7 to focus on competitive road cycling, but picked up running again in 2007 and now competes in duathlons, both locally and regionally. Sadly, a running related injury spelt the end of her dream to represent Singapore in the 2007 SEA Games in the duathlon, but she continues to strive to do her best.

Associate Professor Lim Chin Leong Fabian received his bachelor and master of science degrees from the University of Oregon and his PhD degree (Kinesiology) from the University of Queensland. He also has an MBA from the University of Surrey in the UK. Dr Lim is a recipient of the Defence Science Scholarship from the Ministry of Defence, Singapore, where he has held various appointments since 1991.

Dr Lim is presently the Programme Director for Combat Protection and Performance, and Head of the Military Physiology Laboratory at the Defence Medical and Environmental Research Institute, DSO National Laboratories. Dr Lim is also an Adjunct Associate Professor at the Yong Loo Lin School of Medicine, National University of Singapore and Adjunct Investigator at the Singapore Institute of Clinical Sciences, A*STAR. He also teaches at the Auckland University of Technology Programme in the Singapore Sports School.

Dr Lim has conducted research on a variety of topics in exercise physiology over the last 18 years. Some of these topics include obesity, load carriage, fitness management, exercise immunology, sport nutrition, hydration and thermoregulation. More recently, Dr Lim has been investigating the effects of immune disturbances in the pathology of heat stroke, where he applies the models in exercise immunology in the mechanism of heat stroke. His work in this area has resulted in the development of the dual pathway model of heat stroke. His research work has been translated into more than 30 academic publications in local and international scientific journals.

Ling Ping Sing graduated from Southern Illinois University of Carbondale in United States with a degree in food and nutrition, and has been a registered dietitian (RN) since 2000. She is an Accredited Dietitian of Singapore (ADS) and a member for the Singapore Nutritionist and Dietetic Association (SNDA). Ping Sing also completed a two-month Health Manpower Development Programme (HMDP) attachment in

Leeds, England on weight management in 2004. She went on to complete a course in sport nutrition for dietitians with Sports Dietitians Australia (SDA) on 2006.

Ping Sing has been with Changi General Hospital (CGH) since 2001. She currently runs sessions at the Changi Sports Medicine Centre and Singapore Sports Medicine Centre, providing dietary intervention for patients on the Weight Management Programme and counseling in sports nutrition.

Ping Sing took up running in 2006, her first running event being the 8 km Women's Outdoor Challenge 2007. She now participates in several running events each year, including the 15 km Passion Run, Mizuno Mt Faber Run, Army Half Marathon and Singapore Standard Chartered Marathon.

Ping Sing, who is a strong believer in using nutrition to enhance sport performance and one's well being, believes that you are what you eat. She is determined to use her skills and knowledge to impact the world around her.

14" **Murugiah Rameshon** is Hwa Chong Institution's Head Coach for middle and long distance running. To date, he has coached a total of 12 national schools' cross country teams, winning championship titles from 1995 to 2009.

Coach Rameshon holds a diploma in physical education (Singapore) from the School of Physical Education and a bachelor of science (Hons) in physical education and sports science from Loughborough University. His research thesis then was on heart rate analysis of the 1,500 m race. In 2008, he obtained a masters in education from the University of Western Australia, where his thesis was on the sports participation trend in a Singapore school.

As a runner, Rameshon achieved the following personal bests from 1989 to 1995:

1,500 m   – 4 min 11 sec (Singapore Open)
3,000 m   – 9 min 03 sec (Singapore)
5,000 m   – 15 min 31 sec (Singapore Open Track and Field Race)
10,000 m – 31 min 46 sec (England)
½ Marathon – 1 hr 10 min 52 sec (Malaysia)
Marathon   – 2 hrs 24 min 22 sec (Thailand, SEA Games), National Record

At age 43, Rameshon is still going strong and won the 2008 Singapore Marathon (local category).

In recognition of his sporting achievements, Rameshon was awarded the Merit award from the Singapore Athletics Association in 1991 and the Singapore Olympic Academy the Roll of Honour in 1998.

15" **Jessie Phua** graduated with bachelor of science (podiatry) in 2000 and went on a three-month Health Manpower Development Programme Fellowship in 2006 at the Center for Lower Extremity Ambulatory Research (CLEAR), Dr William M Scholl College of Podiatric Medicine, at Rosalind Franklin University of Medicine & Science. She is the senior podiatrist at the Changi Sports Medicine Centre in Changi General Hospital. Her particular areas of interest are biomechanics, sports injuries, and biomechanics of diabetic feet for exercise and limb preservation. Jessie jogs, swims, cycles, and enjoys nature treks.

16" **Ben Swee** is a personal trainer whose passion for running began in 1997 whilst he was serving the army as part of his national service, leading him to complete his first marathon in that same year. Upon returning to Singapore after completing his bachelor of commerce at the University of Western Australia in 2000, Ben began participating in more local and overseas races of various distances, fueling his passion in both health and fitness. Inspired to fulfill his personal goal to help people achieve their personal health and fitness goals, Ben went on to attain certification in the Singapore Sports Council's Basic Exercise Course and the Federation of International Aerobic and Fitness (FISAF)'s Fitness Leader and Personal Trainer Course. Ben has since completed 18 marathons, an 84km Ultramarathon and several triathlons, including three Ironman events.

17" **Dr Tan Peh Khee** graduated from the National University of Singapore (NUS), Faculty of Medicine, with bachelor of medicine, bachelor of surgery in 2000. He achieved the Membership of Royal College of Surgeons (Edinburgh) in 2006 and was awarded the masters of medicine in orthopaedic surgery in 2007. His main interests are in sports medicine and general orthopaedics.

An avid distance runner, Peh Khee represented his schools (Raffles Junior College, NUS) in long distance track events and cross-country races. His interest in running was first nurtured when he was introduced to cross-country running while at Raffles Junior College. He further pursued his interests by completing six full marathons, numerous triathlons while at medical school and also completed the Singapore Aviva Half Ironman in 2007. He iz also a member of MacRitchie Runners' 25 (MR25), a local long-distance running club.

18" **Philip Tan** is one of the few qualified sports scientists in Singapore having graduated with a bachelor of sports science (with distinction) from Edith Cowan University, Perth, Western Australia. His outstanding academic achievements placed him in the top 10 per cent of the entire university and membership in the prestigious Golden Key International Honors Society.

For the past two years, Philip worked with national elite athletes of both endurance and team sports at the exercise physiology unit of the Singapore Sports Council. He is currently working at the Changi Sports Medicine Centre as an exercise physiologist-cum-head strength & conditioning coach, whose work involves the development and implementation of sports performance testing (particularly for endurance athletes) as well as rehabilitation of injured athletes to prepare them to return to competitive sports.

Philip is also a passionate long distance runner, having completed numerous road races ranging from 10 km to cross-country ultra-marathons of 64 km. With a running/racing experience of slightly over four years, he has contributed much to the local running scene by conducting free running workshops and fitness testing for recreational endurance athletes. For this, he was awarded the Sporting Singapore Inspirational Award 2007 (Youth Category — Commendation Class).

19" **Tan Wei Leong** is a full time running coach who is registered with the Singapore Sports Council's (SSC) National Registry of Coaches (NROC), having obtained the levels 1, 2, and 3 (Theory) certificates under the SSC's National Coaching Accreditation Programme (NCAP). In addition, coach Tan also holds Level 1 (General) and Level 2 (Sprint and Hurdles) coaching certificates issued by the International Amateur Athletic Federation (IAAF), graduating consistently among the top three coaches in these courses.

In 2006 and 2007, Wei Leong was awarded the National Coach Recognition Award in the Development Coaching category by the SSC for his sterling efforts in coaching and mentoring school athletes.

Coach Tan believes there are invaluable life lessons to be experienced in the process of training well, and competing at one's highest personal level. He believes that athletics made his life meaningful.

20" **Dr Roger Tian Ho-Heng** graduated from the National University of Singapore in 1996 and obtained his postgraduate training and qualifications in surgery from the Royal College of Surgeons of Edinburgh. He obtained his masters of sports medicine from the University of New South Wales in 2007 and is an American College of Sports Medicine certified exercise specialist. He has been working at the Changi Sports Medicine Centre for the past four years. He has also worked at the High Performance Division of the Singapore Sports Council, participating in the care of the country's top athletes, and is currently a member of its Human Research Ethics Committee.

Despite his hectic schedule, Dr Tian is active in research and teaching, and has authored several articles in peer-reviewed journals. He contributes regularly to the press and sits on the advisory panel of a local publication. He has served as medical director for past editions of the OSIM Singapore International Triathlon and the inaugural AVIVA 70.3 Singapore Half-Ironman. He runs 40 – 50 km per week, participating in two to three endurance events annually.

INTRODUCTION
>>With input from Darren Leong

ORIGINS OF THE MARATHON

The full marathon, a 42.195 kilometre (km) road race, holds a special draw for many. The race was born at the inaugural 1896 modern Olympics in Athens, to mark the epic 25-mile journey by a Greek messenger from the coastal plain of Marathon to Athens. The messenger, Phidippides, was delivering the news of the Greek victory over the Persians in 490 B.C. He apparently collapsed and died after delivering the news, but the marathon lives on.

The race distance varied until 1921, when the International Amateur Athletic Federation (IAAF) decided to set the 42.195 km distance of the 1908 London Olympics as the standard distance for all marathon races. The 1924 Paris Olympics marathon course was thus the first race officially contested in the current standard distance.

In Singapore, the first full-length marathon was held in 1982 with 2,832 entrants for the 42.195 km race. Raymond Crabb of the United Kingdom and Winnie Ng from Hongkong were the overall men's and women's winners respectively. Goh Gam Seng and Lim Hui Pheng won the local men and women's categories.

In 1984, the Singapore International Marathon was inaugurated and installed as a biennial international marathon. In 1985, Mobil, an oil company, launched the Mobil Marathon, which was held in the years alternating with the Singapore International Marathon and dedicated to the local running community.

In 2002, the Singapore Marathon became the Standard Chartered Singapore Marathon, and continues to be an annual event attracting both international and local participants. Attendance at the marathon has increased exponentially from its early years, with a record number of 50,000 runners taking to the streets in 2008. Of these 15,000 ran the full marathon. The current course record is 2:13:01, by Luke Kibet of Kenya. The Singapore National record holders for the marathon are M Rameshon (1995, Men, 2:24:22) and Yvonne Danson (1995, Women, 2:34:41). Since 2007, the Sundown Marathon, which starts at midnight, was added to the running calendar.

A PERSONAL JOURNEY

I was not much of a runner when I first decided to take running on as a sport. I was a sailor, and most of the physical activity demanded by sailing (in the Laser class in particular) involved hiking out (leaning as far out and away from the midline of the boat as possible to counter the heeling forces generated by the sail), and pulling on the sheets (ropes) that control the sail. In that sense, sailing is more of a strength sport, rather than an aerobic sport. The aerobic demands are only moderate, so Laser sailors spend 60 – 70 per cent of their physical training time on weight training and the rest on cardiovascular training. The cardiovascular training that best simulates the demands of sailing is rowing, followed by cycling, and finally running. Needless to say, I spent minimal time running, and only did so when I could not row or cycle.

The optimal weight for Laser sailors is between 78 and 82 kilogrammes (kg) and I spent six days a week in the gym to bulk up from 64 kg to 78 kg at the peak of my sailing. After I retired from sailing in 1996, I continued to keep fit, mostly by doing weights as I thought it would be a waste to

Ben Tan hiking out on the Laser at the 1996 Olympic Games

lose all the muscle bulk that I painstakingly accumulated during my sailing years.

I was always intrigued with the marathon. In sailing, each race takes about an hour to complete, so I wondered how these runners kept going non-stop for more than double the duration of a sailing race? Could the human body take it? What happens to their bones, tendons, and muscles when subjected to such long hours of torture? What kind of mental strength did they need? What went on in the minds of the great marathoners, during training and competition?

Out of curiosity, I decided to enter my first marathon in November 2002, at the Johor-Singapore Second Link Bridge Run. I was 35 years old then. In the first few editions of the run, they had a full marathon category, and runners would run across the second link, from Singapore to Malaysia and back. I had driven across the second link to Malaysia once before, and I thought it would be easy because the journey by car was a pretty smooth ride. I was curious to see if I had the mental tenacity to complete a full marathon. I was still fairly fit then, so for me it was a test of mental strength — I had not done much competitive sailing for some time, and I wanted to know if I were still mentally strong. And to ensure that it was a test of mental strength, I did not train for the marathon! That turned out to be a huge mistake.

The drive into Malaysia (traffic jams aside) via the second link is a smooth one. Unfortunately, the converse is true when crossing it on foot. When you are in a car, you do not realize that there are no trees or shade on the wide highway, and what is a gentle upslope in a car may not be as gentle when you are on foot! The race turned out to be a mammoth struggle. I hit the proverbial wall way before the 30 km mark. The sun was blazing, it was sweltering, and it was all compounded by the heat emanating from the road. I was so dehydrated that I had stopped perspiring, and had to slow down to a walk. And it was not even a brisk walk as my feet were killing me. I felt faint and my body was tingling all over, and if I attempted to step up the pace, I felt I that would collapse. I recalled a friendly Malaysian lady in her twenties cruising along, passing me at a steady pace, still jogging. When she passed me, she encouragingly said to me in Mandarin, "Let's do it together, just stay with me." I tried, but dropped off barely three minutes later. The 'sweeper' bus started to pick up the stragglers as it was nearing the cutoff time of six hours. As the bus came up behind me, I was tempted to get on, but I pushed on, reminding myself that this was meant to be a test of mental strength. I eventually finished the race, in 5 hours 35 minutes! It was so hot by then that most of the stragglers had not bothered to complete the race and the officials at the finish line had begun to pack the remaining certificates and medals into carton boxes. I came in so late that they had to reopen a box to give me my medal and certificate!

Yes, I proved I had mental strength, but what a price I had to pay! I could barely make my way home after that. After the race, I conducted a postmortem. I was happy that I had still had the mental strength, but the more important revelation was that I had failed physically. To be holistic, we need to develop our mind and body — I passed the mental test, but not the physical one. It was then that I decided to do some more marathons, but this time the challenge was to transform my body into a lean running machine.

That was the start of my systematic preparation towards being a faster marathoner. I set targets, drew up training schedules and training cycles, monitored my training and progress. I had to morph my body from the Incredible Hulk to Spider-Man; from one suited to a sport that favoured strength and muscle bulk, to the polar opposite where lighter is better. I switched from a non-impact sport to a high-impact one.

I whittled my weight down to 64 kg. I remember chugging up steep slopes along my weekday running route, but as I got fitter, I slowly began to jog up those slopes, and not long after, I was running over the hills without even thinking of them. I had lots of help along the way, with experienced runners like Roy Ang and the MacRitchie 25 runners, as well as Lua Choon Huat teaching me the ropes. Running in a group helps, especially for long runs. Choon Huat would go to the extent (and I needed it) of giving me wake up calls at 4 AM so that I would make it on time for our Sunday morning 5 AM long runs.

The initial progress was great — I was setting new personal bests with each marathon, shaving chunks off my finishing time with each effort. My marathon times fell from 5:35 to 3:57, 3:45, 3:30, and 3:21 in the space of three years. Not only that, I realized I was not limping or half-dead after each race — I could still go out for lunch and shopping the same day, and go to work the next day as if the previous day was just a training run. I could see and feel the transformation.

But it was not smooth sailing all the way. In the initial years, because I was not used to the high impact of running, I developed stress fractures in my fibula — three to be exact, one after another. Fortunately, I detected them early and thankfully the fibula is not the worst place to have a stress fracture. I did not have to pay a high price for the fractures, but nevertheless, I learnt from my mistakes and made adjustments to my training programme. Now I run much higher mileages and have not incurred stress fractures for the past few years. Another injury I sustained was a plantar fasciitis, a painful condition involving the bottom of the heel. Again, I detected it early, cut my mileage by 40 per cent, treated it, corrected the underlying causes, and was able to ramp up to the usual mileage within two weeks. I am now running much higher mileages varying between 80 – 120 km, and have not had an injury for the past three years.

While on a Singapore Airlines flight, I chanced upon a 2005 Korean blockbuster that was simply entitled *Marathon*. The hilarious and inspiring true story was about an autistic boy, Cho Won, who aspired to race in the Chuncheon Marathon. He succeeded. It was from the movie that the sub-3 target of completing a marathon in under three hours — the amateur runner's equivalent of an Olympic dream — stuck in my head. I knew that to do a sub-3, it would take some serious training.

En route to a sub-3, I wanted to do the 2007 Boston Marathon — the world's oldest marathon. To qualify, I had to record a 3:15 finish in a certified marathon, and I picked the 2006 Ohtawara Marathon in Japan. Ohtawara is known for its consistently cool weather and relatively flat course. Just before I left for Japan, an old friend of mine, Kwang Min, gave me a book entitled *Ultramarathon Man: Confessions of an All-Night Runner* by Dean Karnazes. I do not usually read anything other than medical literature, as I am always behind on my "to read" list of medical journals. But I brought Kwang Min's book along with me and read it on the plane. I was riveted and finished the book in tears — it was that motivational. As I ran the Ohtawara Marathon, scenes and lines from the book flashed through my mind repeatedly, and kept me going. I finished the race in 3:14:59! It was a very close shave, and if it were not for Kwang Min's gift, I don't think I would have qualified for Boston. I knew that for my level of fitness at that time, I had given everything I had during the race and was exhausted after that. But the satisfaction of having run to the very best of my ability more than made up for the exhaustion. Immediately after the race, our group of runners made our way to the nearby Shiobara onsen district for a heavenly dip in the hot springs. While soaking in natural springs, all I could think of then was, "I deserve and earned this!" (My wife, Alison, read Dean Karnazes' book after seeing me tear over it, concluded that it was written by a madman, but I bought several copies and gave them to my friends and colleagues for Christmas, eager to share the madness.) I made my pilgrimage to Boston and experienced the infamous 'Heartbreak Hill,' deafening cheers of the Wellesley College 'scream tunnel,' 4 – 6 °C temperatures, rain, and chilling winds to finish in 3:19.

After registering the 3:21 in the 2005 Melbourne Marathon, I hit a plateau. My times hovered between 3:24 and 3:12 in the next two years. My dream of doing a sub-3 seemed unattainable — there is a huge gap between 3:12 and 2:59. A runner once told me that I had reached my peak and this was all I could expect. A former runner added that at my age (late 30s), I would not even be able to smell a sub-3. As I wondered if I should just accept reality, I had a flashback to my mid teens, when I was pondering which class of boat I should sail after graduating from the Optimist class, a category reserved for under-15 age group sailors. I was eyeing the Laser class. There are many classes of boats in sailing, but the prestigious ones were the seven or so Olympic classes. Among the Olympic classes, the Laser was considered the 'glamour event', much like the men's singles event in tennis or badminton. The older sailors said that the Laser class was too competitive and I would be better off sailing a less competitive class of boat so that I would at least have a chance at winning something. I thought hard and eventually was guided by what American sailor, Buddy Melges, said, "It is better to be tenth in a word class fleet, than to be first in a mediocre fleet." Competition and challenges are what make us stronger and better, whether we win or not. Ultimately, what is more important than winning is character and self-development. Ultimately, my willingness to face the competition and take on challenges was rewarded with an Asian Games gold, four consecutive Southeast Asian Games golds, and a top 50 ranking in the world. Medals and titles were only the by-product of my drive to discover my potential. I have never turned away from a challenge, and facing my challenges have always made me a better person, whether I won or not. So why should I shy away from pursuing a sub-3 now? Even if I did not go under three hours, the lessons I learnt along the way would be invaluable.

I made up my mind not to give up trying for a sub-3. My training buddies believed in me and encouraged and motivated me, so I persisted. I intensified my training and increased my mileage. But I knew that to make a breakthrough, simply running more was not the answer — I was working full time and had other responsibilities. I drew the line at running six days a week, with one training session a day. I was not willing to go beyond that, to seven days of training and two sessions a day, so I had to train smart, going for quality instead of quantity.

With the smarter training programme, I got better results and began to feel that the sub-3 was within sight, based on my training times. I was going faster than a sub-3 pace on my weekday 16 km runs, and was not even feeling tired after that. I was also recording decent times for my 38 km runs on Sundays. I was handling a mileage of 100 km per week with ease. I thought the Berlin Marathon, with its fast course and perfect temperatures, would be the one where I would finally go under three hours. My hopes were high — until I was hit with dengue fever five weeks before Berlin! For five days, I was floored. I had bad headaches, and my bones and muscles ached badly. I was breathless just getting out of bed. I lost my appetite, and despite forcing myself to eat, my weight dropped to 61 kg in a week, from my usual 63 – 64 kg. I feared I had lost muscle mass, which I needed for the power and speed to do a sub-3. Hoping for some consolation, I called my friend and national thrower, James Wong, who also had dengue fever a few years earlier. "After nine months, I was performing at 80 per cent of my usual self," said James. With the Berlin Marathon only a month away that was not what I wanted to hear. I didn't have nine months to recover. I just had to make the best of the hand that I had been dealt. The first two weeks after I resumed training were discouraging — my training partner, Benny, left me way behind and had already finished and showered by the time I completed the training run at East Coast Park. I was so far behind that I even contemplated taking a cab back my car, where we started our run. Fortunately, my pace recovered pretty quickly after that. My appetite was voracious. I was pleased with the speed at which I bounced back, and was achieving pre-dengue pace by the time I left for Berlin. I was back in the running.

The 2008 Berlin Marathon started with a slight hitch. The corrals were not well policed, and I was caught in a jam after the gun went off. It took me 3 km before I could get into smooth traffic and keep good pace. I was cruising quite effortlessly and the time check at every kilometre was exactly as planned. At 35 km, I was feeling tired and started to struggle, but I kept pace. At the 42 km marker, I was 20 seconds ahead of the 3:00 marathon pace. Despite the pain, I smiled at the thought of doing a sub-3. That was when my pacing fell apart. My legs could not maintain the pace, and when I tried to pick up the pace, I started feeling faint. Turning round the final corner, I could see the finishing line in the distance. I knew it was going to be close, but the harder I tried to speed up, the more I felt like I was going to faint. My body stopped taking orders from my brain, and my brain itself was not working properly. As I crossed under the historic Brandenburg Gate, with the finish line only 400 metres (m) away, my heart sank — my watch indicated that it was three hours. I crossed the line in 3:01. I blew it, all in the last 2 km! As if I wasn't downtrodden enough, my calf started cramping a few minutes after crossing the finishing line. The cramps then spread uncontrollably to my other calf, thighs, arms, and the rest of my body, including my facial muscles! I was stretchered to the medical tent, where the excruciating cramps kept migrating from one muscle group to another for a whole hour. After the cramps abated, it took me an additional 90 minutes to gingerly limp back to the hotel, just 1 km away!

For the next few days, I was in disbelief. The images of the finishing line just 400 m away kept playing back in my head, torturing me. My confidence was again shaken — if I could not do a sub-3 in Berlin, on the course where world records are broken and new ones set, where else could I do it? (In fact, I was running in the very same marathon where Haile Gabrselassie set the current world record time of 2:03:59.)

After the race, the Singaporean runners who were at the Berlin Marathon met for dinner. That was when I first I met Coach Rameshon, the Singapore national record holder for the marathon. His personal best of 2:24, set in 1995, still stands to this day. I was feeling dejected, but he was confident that I could go under three hours in the Singapore Marathon two months away, and invited me to train with him and Daniel Ling, the 2007 Singapore Marathon champion in the local men's category. It was an honour and although I was sure that I would not do a sub-3 at the Singapore Marathon, the opportunity to train and learn from the best was too enticing. After a two week break, I started training with Rameshon and Daniel. Their training was intensive, with tempo runs and hill work. I began to feel a difference — my legs grew stronger and I had newfound speed that I never knew was in me. The Hwa Chong Institution boys (where Rameshon teaches physical education) trained with us, and boy, did they push me hard!

At the 2008 Singapore Marathon, I had a smooth start. I felt strong, and had to hold myself back and stick to the race pace. At the 21 km mark, I had built up a four-minute buffer and was feeling comfortable. At 32 km, I was not struggling, and that felt unusual. Five kilometres from the finish, my legs were still 'listening to orders' — usually, at that stage, they would have a mind of their own and I could not command them to go faster. With 2 km to go, I was getting worried as things were going too well — I had never felt that strong at that stage of the race before, and whatever buffer I had built up usually would have dwindled away long before. I still had the four-minute buffer that I had built up early in the race. Would Murphy's Law strike once again? No! Amazingly, I crossed the line in 2:56; I felt so contented that all the hard work paid off. I would have been happy with a 2:59, but a 2:56 in Singapore's hot, humid weather! I was glad I had not given up hope of doing a sub-3. And I achieved it at the age of 41. To top it off,

Run for your Life!

28

after I crossed the line, Rameshon and Daniel ran back towards me and informed me that I had finished third! That meant that we had a 1-2-3 finish! Teamwork — never underestimate its power. We trained as a team; we succeeded as a team!

Throughout this eye-opening journey of self-discovery, I took full advantage of my experience as an international Laser sailor, my background in sports medicine and sports science, and the members of Singapore's running fraternity. I soaked up information and processed the information, discarding the myths and putting into practice the accurate facts. I experimented with training methodologies and philosophies using myself as the guinea pig. At times, I had to learn things the hard way. But I had fun along the way and will always be indebted to Roy Ang, Goh Aik Guan, Lua Choon Huat, David Tay, Benny Goh, Daniel Ling, Rameshon, and many others for their encouragement and company. It is a rewarding journey that promises gratification, albeit delayed. With more and more Singaporeans taking up running, my wish is to share what others have taught me, so that more runners can realize their personal dreams in a safe and structured manner.

From left to right, Daniel Ling, Ben Tan, and M Rameshon celebrating their 1-2-3 finish at the 2008 Singapore Marathon

JOIN THE CLUB

Roy Ang was an unfit 78 kg when he started running in 1986. While running at the MacRitchie Reservoir Park, Roy was invited by fellow runners to join their club, the MacRitchie Runners 25 (MR25). "I got the motivation to continue running because of the group. It gave me a target, and the group shared their running tips with me. MR25 also organizes many running activities, including the progressive runs that culminate in the year-end marathon," says an appreciative Roy.

Fifty-year-old Roy recalls, "I started running to lose weight, but later I got hooked onto running." He is now 56 kg. And in 1989, just three years after joining MR25, Roy recorded his personal best marathon time of 2:56 hours (hr) in New Zealand Force Marathon. To this day, Roy will put runners half his age to shame in any marathon.

It was Roy who first showed me the ropes when I started running. Roy was much faster than me, but he would slow down to run by my side and encourage me all the way to the finish. Even after so many years, you can count on Roy and the other MR25 runners to be at MacRitchie on Sunday mornings, if you need company on your long runs.

The MR25 was formed in 1976 and has a good mix of runners of all ages. If you are wondering how the name came about, the answer is in the 5 km (4.8 km for women) cross-country time trial that you have to undergo before joining as a member. If you can do it under 25 minutes, then welcome to the Club! But don't worry — everyone is very friendly and I was welcomed and running with the group for a long time before I eventually attempted and cleared the time trial.

Apart from the MR25, there are many other running groups in Singapore, some bigger, some smaller. There are even clubs with names like Team FatBird and ABC. Whichever one you decide to hook up with, you will see why running is such a social and popular sport.

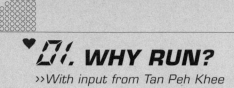

01. WHY RUN?

>>*With input from Tan Peh Khee*

HEALTH BENEFITS OF RUNNING

What better way to exercise than running? Human beings evolved to walk and run more than 4 million years ago when we rose from all fours. We were made to run — 10,000 years ago, hunter-gatherers like the Tarahumara Indians in Mexico, ran many miles a day on the hunt. In 490 B.C., Pheidippides, an ancient "day-runner" put running on the world map when he ran 149 miles to carry the news of the Persian landing at Marathon to Sparta in order to enlist help for the battle.

Running strengthens the heart by making it a more powerful pump. It lowers blood pressure, improves the level of good (HDL) cholesterol, reduces the level of the bad (LDL) cholesterol, and minimizes the risk of stroke and heart attack. Running maintains the elasticity of the arteries because they expand and contract three times as much as usual when a person runs. Running also improves lung function as 50 per cent of the normally unused lungs are utilized during running.

In addition, as running is a weight-bearing exercise, the stress it places on the skeletal system through pounding against the ground causes an increase in the bone mineral density. This minimizes the risk of osteoporosis and fractures. The psychomotor training that trail running provides also improves the muscular coordination of the body. This helps to minimize the risks of falls in the elderly and further contributes to the reduction of fractures sustained from falls.

Many people actually start running in order to stay slim or combat obesity. Studies have shown that approximately 60 per cent of runners start running to maintain their weight. Running is one of the top activities for burning fat. With the exception of cross-country skiing, running burns more calories per minute than any other cardiovascular exercise, due to the large muscle groups that are mobilized. The successful treatment of obesity has been shown to reduce the risk of type II diabetes mellitus, obstructive sleep apnoea, fatty liver, cancers (e.g. of the colon, breast, uterus, ovary, prostate), subfertility (decreased chances of getting pregnant), and varicose veins.

Running has even been purported to retard the aging process. It does this by slowing the muscle and bone loss that tend to occur with age. Running also promotes the release of human growth hormone, which is thought to maintain the general physical well-being of a person. Maximal aerobic capacity (a measure of the body's ability to use and transport oxygen during exercise, also known as $\dot{V}O_{2max}$) is thought to decline by 10 per cent per decade, starting from the mid-20s. In my twenties, I had a maximal aerobic capacity of 56 ml/kg/min; now at the

AGE IS NO BARRIER

Ronnie Wong only started running at the age of 34 years, when he moved from Singapore to Bermuda in 1980. He was then working as a chef and regularly hung out at discos till 4 AM. A friend bet him six shots of whiskey that he could not finish a 10 km race. He won his bet and got hooked on running — so hooked that he even ran a marathon in Bermuda the day after his wedding in 1988 and won, making headline news. Ronnie has since stopped drinking, realizing that it was neither helping his health nor his running. He does not have any of the medical problems that often plague those his age, and still leads a disease-free life. Now 63 years old and living in Maryland,

Ronnie Wong (centre), together with (behind, from left to right) Ben Tan, David Tay, and Lua Choon Huat, after a Sunday morning run.

USA, Ronnie continues to run in marathons and ultramarathons. Is age slowing Ronnie down? "Of course not. I think I'm getting faster," retorted the man who has been recording sub-3:30 marathon times in very recent years. In 2008, he completed his 200th marathon!

Kor Hong Fatt (*right*) was 70 years old when he suffered a heart attack. Following that wake-up call, Hong Fatt started running regularly at the age of 71 years. "I had to be fit. I had to take care of myself, so that I can take care of her," he says, referring to his wife, who suffered a stroke in 1994. "We can't be a burden to our children," added the father of two married sons. Hong Fatt finished his first marathon in 2003, and later set his personal best marathon time of 4:47:30. Now, at age 77, he has completed 10 marathons, and plans to continue running till he is 80. "It's all about knowing your body well and listening to it," replies Hong Fatt, when asked about how he manages to keep going.

age of almost 42 years, my maximal aerobic capacity has increased to 70 ml/kg/min when it should have declined by 20 per cent. Thanks to running, I have managed to cheat time!

Running is not only good for our bodies, it is also good for our minds. "Running causes animals' brains to produce markedly more brain cells in the hippocampus, the part of the brain involved in learning and memory," says Dr Ho New Fei, a postdoctoral fellow with the Functional Brain Imaging Laboratory, National University of Singapore. She conducts research on exercise and brain function, and adds that, "Running also increases the capacity of brain cells to communicate with one another, and improves the animal's performance in a spatial memory task. In humans, aerobic training is linked to a significant increase in brain volume and activity in the parts of the brain associated with executive functions, such as decision-making and problem-solving."

We also know that running can relieve stress in a person's life and bring about the runner's euphoria through the release of natural endorphins, a hormone similar to morphine. Hence, most people feel and function better after a run than before it, prompting psychologists to prescribe running to combat mild depression. Long runs are great at affording space and time for a person to think through a problem. More importantly, running promotes positive thinking and builds confidence in a person. In a runner who is into serious training, running can also imbibe a sense of discipline which is applicable to other areas of life, be it work or academic pursuit

THE CHALLENGE

So, we all know running is good for us, but why 42.195 km? There are races covering anything from a 100 m sprint to middle distance races to half marathons. The big difference is that, unless we train for it, we do not have enough energy stores to run continuously for 42 km. We tend to hit the wall from about 25 km onwards, when we run out of carbohydrates stores and have to slow down because our fat stores cannot be mobilized as quickly. If you are able to do a 10 km run, it is not much harder to do a 21 km run. But from 21 km to 42 km, it is a different story! The pain is not two-fold, but disproportionately more. Hence, the marathon is distinctly different from shorter distances because the distance extends beyond what we would usually have in our fuel tanks. It requires prolonged training and the biochemical adaptations that it induces, in order to complete the last 10 or so kilometers. It is precisely the difficulty of completing 42.195 km that makes the marathon the Everest for most runners.

Another draw of the marathon is the delayed gratification. We know it is not a race that one can simply grit his teeth and complete — it requires months of dedicated training. Not only do we have to train our musculockclctal systems to tolerate the high impact and our cardiovascular systems to deliver adequate oxygen and fuel to our muscles, but we also have to teach our bodies to use the fuel efficiently in order to last the distance and finish in one piece.

In a marathon, you are racing against yourself. Unlike races of shorter distances, most people do not care if they come in 50th or 5,000th; it is more about achieving a time target that you have set for yourself. There is great personal triumph and satisfaction in breaking that five, four or three hour barrier. To hit your target, not only must you be adequately prepared, but you also need a sound race plan and execute it to perfection.

I DID IT FOR MY GIRL!

After I tore the lateral meniscus of my right knee in 2002, I had difficulty with speed training. I then decided to channel my dreams to marathon running where speed was not crucial. First, I set the target of winning the Singapore Marathon men's closed (local) category. With a 10 km time of 32 min and a 21 km time of 1 hr 15 min, I won the 2004 Singapore Marathon men's closed category in 2 hr 45 min 03 sec. The win motivated me to make it two in a row in 2005.

As no Singaporean had ever won three consecutive Singapore Marathons before, I yearned for the hat trick. Number three would not be easy, as my knees were getting in the way of my training, and I was struggling.

On 14 May 2006, my wife gave birth to a beautiful baby girl. That made me forget about my knees and motivated me to train hard. During the 2006 race itself, the vision of me standing on the winner's podium with my daughter in my arms carried me kilometre after kilometre to the finishing line. And with it, my dream of winning three Singapore Marathons in a row became reality.

Anything is possible if you find a reason to do it!

G. Elangovan
Former National middle distance runner
Running coach
Three-time winner of the local men's category of the Singapore Marathon

One does not become a marathoner overnight. Endurance running requires an extended period of training. The training provides a stimulus to induce adaptations in our bodies to make us more efficient runners.

Let us first understand how our body works when we run. They are all related, but I'd like to simplify things by looking at the four key systems that enable us to run: the musculoskeletal, energy, cardiorespiratory, and cooling systems.

BODY SYSTEMS
Musculoskeletal system

Running comprises a series of coordinated movements involving our musculoskeletal system, which comprises our muscles, tendon, bones, and joints. Tendons, which are slightly elastic structures, serve to attach our muscles to bones, while ligaments join one bone to another. Muscles contain contractile elements that require energy to contract. Hence, contracting muscles move our limbs much like a lever. For example, the quadriceps muscles in the front of the thigh help to flex the hip and extend the knees as we run, while the hamstring muscles at the back of the thigh do the opposite.

Each muscle fibre is a cell, containing the active actin and myosin that contract using energy supplied by adenosine triphosphate (ATP). Mitochondria, the cell's powerhouses, generate ATP from fat and carbohydrate, using oxygen that is brought there from the surface of the cell by myoglobin. The oxygen is brought to the muscle fibre by haemoglobin in the blood vessels, the smallest of which are capillaries that surround each muscle fibre. Motor nerves interface with the muscle fibres via motor end plates. Our brain and spinal cord control movements by sending electrical impulses down these nerves to trigger muscle contractions (see figure 2.1).

Your endurance and speed during the run depend largely on your muscles' ability to produce energy and force.

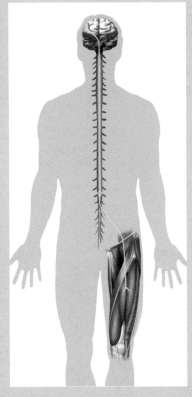

Figure. 2.1. Impulses generated in the brain and spinal cord are transmitted via motor nerves to the muscles, triggering a series of coordinated muscle contractions to bring about movement.

Generally, there are two main types of muscle fibres existing in various proportions within the muscles. These fibres are differentiated on the basis of their colour, the quantity of mitochondria they contain, and the speed at which they contract. Type 1 or Slow-twitch (ST) fibres are red and have a high concentration of mitochondria and myoglobin. On the other hand, Type II or Fast-twitch (FT) fibres are white and have low mitochondrial content. ST muscle fibres are very efficient at producing ATP from the oxidation of carbohydrates and fat and are recruited most often during endurance events such as the marathon. FT muscle fibres, while able to generate more force than ST fibres, fatigues easily due to their limited endurance and are hence recruited mainly for explosive sprinting events.

The bones and joints are an important part of the skeletal system. These structures are subject to substantial impact forces as we run. Even while jogging, the impact forces that reverberate through our skeletal system are about three times our bodyweight.

Energy Systems

When we run, muscles contract and relax in a coordinated pattern to propel the body forward. This work requires energy, which is provided to the muscles in the form of ATP.

ATP is generated from carbohydrate or fat via the aerobic (i.e. requiring oxygen) or anaerobic (i.e. no oxygen needed) system. The latter comprises the ATP-phosphocreatine system and the anaerobic lactic system. There are therefore three energy systems that deliver ATP to the working muscles:

1. The ATP-PC (Adenosine-Triphosphate Phosphocreatine) system is the instant energy source as it relies on existing ATP that is stored in the muscle cells. When energy is needed immediately, phosphates are split from ATP molecules to release energy. However, this system can only last up to 10 seconds before the ATP runs out, and is at work when you push for a short sprint.

2. The anaerobic lactic system breaks down carbohydrate or fat to produce ATP when the exercise intensity is high. It can generate ATP in the absence of oxygen, but lactic acid (lactate) is generated as a by-product. As our body can only tolerate a certain amount of lactate accumulation, we cannot rely on the anaerobic lactic system beyond two to three minutes.

3. The aerobic system is the most important for endurance athletes, as it is a sustainable and efficient source of ATP. Unlike the anaerobic lactic system, the aerobic system requires oxygen to produce ATP from carbohydrate or fat.

All three energy systems are active concurrently, but the contribution varies according to the intensity and duration of your run (figure 2.2).

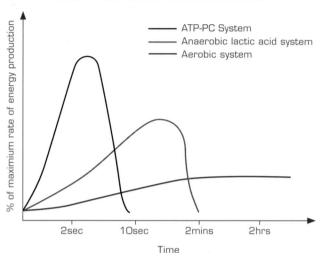

ENERGY SYSTEMS DURING EXERCISE

Figure 2.2. The ATP-PC system is the main source of energy for short bursts of activity lasting up to 10 s. The anaerobic lactic acid system is activated during high-intensity activity lasting two to three minutes. The aerobic system can be relied on for longer durations, but the rate of energy production is low, and oxygen is required.

There are three main energy sources or substrates, namely carbohydrates, fat, and proteins. Carbohydrates are our body's first-choice fuel, as it is fast-release. Carbohydrates (e.g. glycogen and glucose) are stored mainly in our liver and muscles, and there is about 2,000 kilocalories (kcal) worth of carbohydrate stores. When we run continuously, we will soon run out of carbohydrates, usually 30 km later, and that is when we 'hit the wall.'

Our other source of fuel is fat. Unlike carbohydrates, our fat stores are practically limitless. Let's say you weigh 70 kg and your body is 20 per cent fat, then you would have 14 kg of fat. This amount of fat contains 107,800 kcal of energy (1 kg of body fat contains 7,700 kcal), whereas we only need about 3,000 kcal to complete a marathon! Unfortunately, the body fat can only be released slowly — at moderate to fast running speeds, we have to depend mostly on carbohydrates.

Proteins, mostly found in muscles, can also be burnt for energy. However, our bodies are reluctant to do this, as we need our muscles, especially if we are physically active. Hence, it is not a major energy source.

Cardiovascular System

The muscles of endurance runners require oxygen and energy substrates. These are delivered to the muscles by the cardiovascular system. Oxygen in inhaled air is brought into contact with blood carried in fine blood vessels (capillaries) within the lungs. As blood passes through the capillaries in the lungs, carbon dioxide (a waste product of energy production) is released and exhaled out of the body. Simultaneously, oxygen is taken up by haemoglobin within our red blood cells. The haemoglobin transports the oxygen from the lungs to all cells and ultimately into the mitochondria for the production of ATP.

While the lung serves as the interface to transfer oxygen from the air to the haemoglobin in our blood, the heart pumps the blood round the body, so that the oxygen from the lungs can reach the muscles. The cardiac output, or the volume of blood that is pumped out of the heart every minute, reflects the effectiveness of this pump. For most individuals, this is about 5 L/min. The cardiac output is dependent on the stroke volume (the amount of blood pumped out with each cardiac contraction) and the heart rate:

$$\text{cardiac output (CO)} = \text{stroke volume (SV)} \times \text{heart rate (HR)}$$

The cardiac output required to feed our muscles is mostly dependent on our running speed. Hence, if two runners are running at the same speed, both will have similar cardiac outputs, but the fitter runner with the more powerful pump (i.e. bigger SV) will have a lower heart rate than the unfit runner. With a lower heart rate, the heart is less taxed at that speed compared to the unfit runner.

Endurance is reflected by one's maximal aerobic capacity, or $\dot{V}O_{2max}$. The $\dot{V}O_{2max}$ is like the engine capacity of a car — the bigger it is, the better, and it is dependent on a few variables, where:

$$\dot{V}O_{2max} = CO \times \text{arteriovenous oxygen difference}$$

The arteriovenous oxygen difference is the difference in oxygen concentration between the blood entering and exiting the muscle, and reflects the muscle's ability to extract oxygen, which, in turn, is dependent on the capillarity (number of capillaries surrounding the muscle) and amount of mitochondria in the muscles.

While is it good to have a large 'engine capacity,' this must be taken in context to the size of the vehicle — having a large engine in a heavy car does not make it a fast car. What you want is a large engine in a light car. Hence, the relevant parameter is not the absolute but the relative $\dot{V}O_{2max}$, where:

$$\text{Relative } \dot{V}O_{2max} = \dot{V}O_{2max} \div \text{bodyweight}$$

Cooling System

Heat production can increase by 10- to 20-fold during intense running. The body is only able to use approximately 25 per cent to 30 per cent of the energy from food to perform physical work, leaving about 70 per cent 'wasted' as heat, which is transported from the muscles to the skin and lungs by circulating blood. The skin and lungs then dissipates the heat to the environment. The regulation of body temperature (thermoregulation) has a significant influence on performance in endurance events. If we are unable to remove the excess heat quickly enough, the high body temperature (approximately 40 °C core temperature) can signal the brain to induce fatigue and compromise running performance. Researchers have observed that faster runners tend to have higher body temperatures at the end of the race than the slower runners, suggesting that the ability to tolerate a high body temperature is beneficial to running performance. Native African runners perform better than Caucasian runners in the heat but not in cool environments. The higher body mass in Caucasians causes their body temperatures to rise faster when running in the heat, which causes these runners to run slower in order to prevent overheating. In contrast, African runners, with lower body mass, have the advantage of lower heat production even when running in the heat. This advantage allows the African to tolerate a higher running pace without overheating.

Apart from heat production by the muscles, another factor that influences body temperature during a run is running economy. An economical runner will expend less energy when running at the same speed as an inefficient runner. Running economy will be discussed in further detail in Chapter 5. The lower energy requirement in the more efficient runner translates into less internal heat production during the run.

The evaporation of sweat accounts for about 80 per cent of heat removed from the body. Evaporation occurs when sweat changes from liquid to gaseous state, and this is facilitated by a low relative humidity. Sweating alone, without evaporation (e.g. sweat dripping off the body), results in fluid loss without significant heat removal. Runners feel more comfortable running in a cooler environment, but do bear in mind that high relative humidity can also exist in cool environment. For example, the relative humidity in Singapore is the lowest at noon (about 60 per cent) and highest at about 1 AM (approximately 90 per cent). The cool environment should not lead to a false sense of security from the effects of heat stress.

Heat stress puts a strain on the cardiovascular system by diverting blood away from the muscles to the skin for heat dissipation. The loss of body water through sweating reduces the circulating blood volume, further taxing the cardiovascular system. Running at moderate to high intensity can induce a sweat rate of approximately 1 – 3 litres (L) per hour. Some electrolytes (salts) are also lost from the body through the sweat. If the sweat loss is not replaced during a long run, the blood volume contracts and compromises the cardiac output. The heart compensates for the lower blood volume (and pressure) by pumping more rapidly in order to maintain blood flow to the muscles so that the run can be sustained. This compensatory increase in heart rate, known as cardiovascular drift, forces the heart to work harder. If the cardiac output cannot be maintained, then running performance is compromised and heat injuries such as heat cramps, heat exhaustion, and heat stroke can occur.

It is important to understand the key systems involved in running because those are the areas we are working on improving during training. You will not progress quickly if you train blindly without understanding what you are doing. Think of the key body systems as analogous to parts of a racecar (figure 2.3):

	Car	Human
❶	Chassis	Musculoskeletal system (muscles, bones and joints)
❷	Fuel Tank	Energy system (carbohydrate and fat stores)
❸	Engine	Cardiovascular system (heart and blood vessels)
❹	Radiator	Cooling system (skin and lungs)

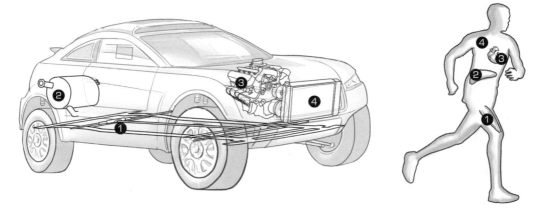

Figure 2.3. Key body systems involved in running and their equivalents in a racecar

TRAINING ADAPTATIONS

The whole purpose of training is to induce adaptations in the four systems we just discussed. Each system and each structure adapts at a different rate. For example, muscle adapts faster than bone. Adaptation takes time and cannot be rushed beyond an optimal rate. For adaptations to occur, there must be a stimulus or stress beyond what the system or structure is accustomed to (i.e. the principle of training overload), and the stimulus must be specific to the system or structure (i.e. the principle of training specificity). For example, cycling, like running, stimulates the cardiovascular system; but it is not specific enough for runners as cycling is non-impact and does not provide the necessary stress to the bones to help it adapt to the impact forces encountered during running. The following are the progressive changes that you benefit from when you run regularly.

Cardiovascular System

The earliest change to occur is the increase in plasma (your blood minus the cellular components) volume. The increased plasma volume is extremely helpful to performance because it leads to an increased stroke volume and hence cardiac output (see formula on page 41). This expansion in plasma volume is detectable within a week of commencing your training. But easy come, easy go, as they say — when you stop training, your plasma volume starts to contract within two days, demonstrating the training principle of reversibility.

The haemoglobin content in the blood also increases, boosting the blood's ability to transport oxygen.

Progressively, your heart's muscle mass increases, in particular the left ventricle, which is the most important part of the pump. Hence, endurance athletes are known to have 'big hearts,' literally. With a more powerful pump, the stroke volume and hence the cardiac output increases, delivering more blood to the working muscles during running.

Musculoskeletal System

One of the most important adaptations is the increase in the number of capillaries surrounding each muscle fibre (i.e. capillarity). This would allow greater exchange of gases, nutrients and waste products between the blood and the working muscle fibres. Myoglobin content within the muscle fibres has also been shown to increase by 75 to 80 per cent, allowing more oxygen to be shuttled from the cell membrane to the mitochondria. Finally, the mitochondria also increase in number, size and efficiency, improving the muscle's capacity to produce ATP.

The muscles also become stronger and more resilient to damage during training. Likewise, the tendons also become stronger, firmly anchoring the muscles to the bone.

Running is a high impact activity. To tolerate such repeated impact, the bones have to become more resilient to the impact, otherwise stress fractures occur. Within our bones, there are microscopic scaffolds that give it its strength. With repeated impact, these scaffolds are able to remodel, whereby they are resorbed (meaning they are broken down and then removed) and new ones form so that the bones can better tolerate the stress lines. The diameter of long bones increases, enabling them to tolerate heavier loads. The mineral content, namely calcium, also increases — that is why impact activities are recommended for the prevention of osteoporosis or loss of bone mass. Bones adapt slower than muscles do,

so we have to build up our mileage gradually — if you have been running 10 km per week, it will take you a few years before you can tolerate a mileage of 100 km per week.

Energy System

It was mentioned earlier that carbohydrates are our main energy source, and we only have a limited carbohydrate store. Fortunately, with consistent training, your liver and muscle will be able to store considerably more glycogen. With a bigger fuel tank, you will be able to run longer.

Another training adaptation is the ability to mobilize fat faster, thus supplementing the energy from carbohydrates. If we are able to better mobilize fat, we then have a lower reliance on carbohydrate during exercise. This carbohydrate-sparing ability can save you from hitting the wall.

These biochemical adaptations are often forgotten despite being crucial for distance runners. These adaptations, brought about by long slow runs, differentiate distance runners from middle distance runners and sprinters.

Cooling System

An improvement in thermoregulation will result in a lower body temperature when running, enabling the runner to exercise longer. Thermoregulation can be improved through a process known as heat acclimatisation. By running in the heat daily for 10 – 14 days, the body can be conditioned to run faster, under hotter environmental conditions. Physiological adaptations can be observed after just three to four days, and minimal adaptations are observed after 14 days.

During heat acclimatisation, sweat rates increase. Hence, training adaptation keeps our temperatures down by producing more, not less, sweat. As the human body has no means of storing water, heat acclimatsed runners need to drink more water to compensate for the increased sweat rates. We are most hydrated at the start of the race, and from there on, we get more and more dehydrated if we do not replace our losses. Hence, hydration strategies during the race are critical for optimal performance.

Electrical impulses travel through our nerves and muscles, and for this electrical system to be stable, the electrolyte (e.g. sodium, potassium, calcium, magnesium) concentration around the nerves and muscles must also be kept within a tight range. For example, hypocalcemia (calcium levels in the blood falling below the normal range) causes our muscles to go into spasms; hyponatraemia (low sodium concentration in the blood) leads to swelling in the brain and induces coma. As the electrolyte concentration is critical to the body's function, our body adapts to regular training by reducing the amount of electrolytes lost through sweating, thus conserving electrolytes.

03. MEASURING YOUR FITNESS PARAMETERS

>>With input from Philip Tan & M Rameshon

This book is about training smart. To take the guesswork out of training, coaches typically conduct field and/or laboratory tests to fine-tune their runners' training programmes. Such tests can benefit both elite and recreational distance runners, and they serve to:

- **To identify weaknesses.** The main purpose is to establish clearly where a runner's strengths and weaknesses lie. This involves identifying the major determinants of distance running performance, measuring them, and then comparing against benchmarks. A training program can then be prescribed to address weaknesses and maintain strengths.

- **To monitor progress and training efficacy.** By repeating appropriate tests at regular intervals, the coach or runner can evaluate the effectiveness of the prescribed training program. Serial testing provides much more information than a one-off test.

- **To predict performance potential.** A number of countries have enjoyed some success at identifying individuals who may be suitable for distance running based on certain antropometric and/or physiological capacities. However, talent identification is never 100 per cent accurate.

Field tests are convenient but less accurate, while the laboratory tests are more sophisticated and costly, but accurate.

FIELD TESTS

The most straightforward field tests are time trials of various distances. Marathon runners often use their 1, 3, 5, 10, 15, and 21 km time trials to predict their full marathon timings and monitor their training progress. Reference tables can be used to project the running time of a particular distance based on the time achieved in another distance. One such useful table is the VDOT table devised by exercise physiologist-cum-coach Jack Daniels in his book, *Daniels' Running Formula* (2nd Ed, 2005, published by Human Kinetics).

Field tests can also be used to predict physiological parameters such as maximal aerobic capacity. Examples include the Cooper and Beep tests. Unfortunately, they provide only gross estimates that are of value in assessing the fitness of the general population and beginner runners; they are not accurate enough for the purpose of fine-tuning the training programmes of elite runners. The better the athlete, the higher the level of accuracy needed.

LABORATORY-BASED PHYSIOLOGICAL TESTS

In the past, laboratory testing was the privilege of elite athletes, but with the technology becoming cheaper and more accessible, recreational runners can benefit from such services as well. Commercial labs are now available, but before running off to get yourself tested, bear in mind that these tests are worth doing only if you know how to interpret and make use of the results. It is important that you have access to an exercise phyciologist, sports physician, or a scientifically oriented coach who will help translate the results to training plans.

Types of Laboratory Tests

Physiological tests can be laboratory- or field-based, direct or indirect, invasive or non-invasive. Laboratory tests have the advantage of a controlled environment whereas field-based tests reflect the competition environment better. A direct test measures the actual physiological characteristic (e.g. measuring $\dot{V}O_{2max}$ for assessing aerobic capacity) whereas an indirect test measures a surrogate of the physiological characteristic (e.g. 2.4 km run to reflect aerobic capacity). Direct tests are more accurate than indirect tests, but tend to be harder to conduct. Invasive tests include biopsies of muscle tissue to determine muscle type, and sampling of blood to measure blood lactate levels. Most tests, such as video gait analysis, are non-invasive.

The Big Four

There are many factors that determine how well a distance runner performs and as many tests that are available. However, the four most useful parameters to measure are maximal oxygen uptake ($\dot{V}O_{2max}$), lactate (anaerobic) threshold, running economy, and video gait analysis. The $\dot{V}O_{2max}$ improves as we get aerobically fitter, up to a genetically determined point. From there, we can still become even faster runners by improving our lactate threshold and running economy.

Maximal Oxygen Uptake ($\dot{V}O_{2max}$), measures our aerobic capacity. $\dot{V}O_{2max}$ refers to the maximum amount of oxygen muscles can use at the highest exercise intensity. This is similar to the engine of a car — the bigger it is, the more fuel it consumes. So if your muscles are capable of using a lot of oxygen, it indicates a higher power output from your muscles. But we need to look at the power output in relation to body mass, as you will not be fast if you install a powerful engine in a lorry as compared to a light-bodied racecar. Hence, for runners, what matters more is the relative $\dot{V}O_{2max}$, which is the absolute $\dot{V}O_{2max}$ divided by the body mass. Elite marathoners have a relative $\dot{V}O_{2max}$ that comfortably exceeds 70 ml/min/kg, compared to the man-on-the-street who has an average relative $\dot{V}O_{2max}$ of 35 ml/min/kg.

While a high $\dot{V}O_{2max}$ may be considered to be a prerequisite for elite performance in distance running, it does not guarantee achievement at the highest level of sport — the $\dot{V}O_{2max}$ can separate the able from the less able but not a gold medallist from a silver medallist.

$\dot{V}O_{2max}$ VERSES TIME

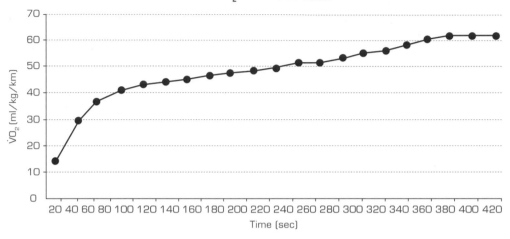

Figure 3.1. As running speed increases, oxygen consumption increases up to a point before it plateaus.

The test is conducted on a treadmill, and the speed and gradient are stepped up in stages until you give up. As you are running, you breathe through a mask, and the metabolic cart or metalyzer measures the amount of oxygen you consume and the carbon dioxide you produce (see figure 3.1). The test will take about 10 minutes to complete, and you are required to go all-out. Other than obtaining the $\dot{V}O_{2max}$, the test also churns out the $v\dot{V}O_{2max}$, i.e. the speed at which you achieved your $\dot{V}O_{2max}$. This is a very useful figure as it accurately identifies the optimal speed for the runner to do his aerobic interval training.

To ensure greater accuracy when measuring your $\dot{V}O_{2max}$, choose direct measurements (as opposed to indirect measurements such as predicting the $\dot{V}O_{2max}$ from heart rates during running trials),

Figure 3.2 Maximal aerobic capacity being determined at the Changi Sports Medicine Centre. An exercise physiologist conducts the test.

use a running protocol (rather than a cycling ergometer), ensure the equipment (called a metalyzer or metabolic cart) is a reputable one, and engage a good exercise physiologist to conduct the test (see figure 3.2).

Lactate Threshold   At high exercise intensities, our muscles produce lactate. We can tolerate excessive lactate accumulation only for short durations, and hence for distance races, we need to run below a certain lactate threshold. The higher the threshold, the higher the running speed we can sustain. During incremental exercise, our blood lactate initially remains at baseline levels (usually less than 2.0 mmol/L), and as running speed increases, we reach a point where the lactate rises significantly above the baseline. This is usually termed lactate threshold 1 (see figure 3.3). As the running speed continues to increase, we reach another critical point where there is a very rapid rise and accumulation of lactate, called the onset of blood lactate accumulation (OBLA).

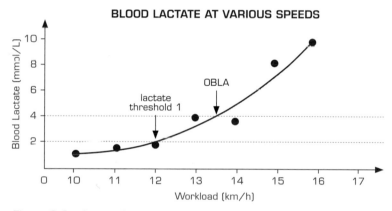

Figure 3.3. *As running speed increases, the lactate increases significantly above the baseline (lactate threshold 1). With a further increase in speed, lactate accumulates quickly in the blood, causing the runner to fatigue (lactate threshold 2 or onset of blood lactate accumulation, OBLA).*

Blood lactate accumulation during incremental exercise tests is commonly used to evaluate the effects of training, to set training intensities and to predict performance. To conduct the test, the runner is required to complete a 30 – 40 minute testing protocol, initially run at a low speed. The speed is then increased by 1 km/hr every five minutes until the runner is unable to continue. Between each stage, the finger is pricked to measure the lactate concentration in the blood. This is plotted against the running speed to obtain the graph seen in figure 3.3.

Unfortunately, there is a lack of consistency in how the test is conducted and interpreted. Exercise physiologists may use different definitions of the lactate threshold, different running protocols, and different methods of obtaining the threshold from the lactate-workload graph.

The data obtained from lactate testing can be used to prescribe intensities for various training purposes. Long runs for building endurance base are usually done below lactate threshold 1. The pace slightly above lactate threshold 1 is also associated with one's marathon race pace. Runs to improve one's lactate tolerance, known as tempo or threshold runs, are usually done at or slightly above the OBLA. The speed between the OBLA and $\dot{V}O_{2max}$ is also utilized to prescribe "cruise intervals" of distances between 1,200 m to 2,000 m.

Running Economy Running economy is typically defined as the energy demand for a given running speed, and is determined by measuring the steady-state consumption of oxygen at various speeds. Taking body mass into consideration, runners with good running economy use less energy and therefore, less oxygen than runners with poor running economy at the same speed. Often quoted as the "forgotten factor of elite running performance", running economy has gained much attention in recent years due to the recognition that it is a better predictor of running performance than even the $\dot{V}O_{2max}$ in elite runners with similar level of aerobic fitness.

The test involves the runner running on a treadmill while the oxygen consumption is measured directly using a metabolic cart. The oxygen consumptions at incremental running speeds (below OBLA) are determined, to obtain the plot below (see figure 3.4):

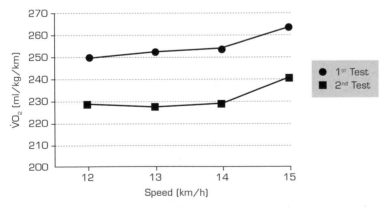

SERIAL RUNNING ECONOMY MEASUREMENTS

Figure 3.4. Running economy of a runner measured on two occasions 10 months apart, showing an improvement in running economy. For the same running speed, the runner requires less oxygen (2ⁿᵈ Test) compared to the earlier test (1ˢᵗ Test).

With serial measurements, you can overlay your current running economy curve over a previous one. If the current curve is below and to the right of the previous one, then your running economy has improved. Running economy is influenced by muscle strength and running technique. See Chapter 5 on how you can improve your running economy.

At the elite level, running economy is usually assessed by looking at the $\dot{V}O_{2max}$ in ml/kg/km at a standardized speed of 16.0 km/hr for male and 14.0 km/hr for female runners (both at 1 per cent treadmill gradient). The average $\dot{V}O_{2max}$ in well-trained male runners at 16 km/hr is 190 ml/kg/km.

Figure 3.5. Video capture from a video gait analysis.

Video Gait Analysis   While a runner is on a treadmill running at race pace, his running gait is captured on video from at least two angles. The video clip is analysed frame-by-frame to look for running faults that may lead to injury or adversely affect running economy. The advantage of analysing gait on video is that more details can be picked up compared to eye-balling. Software can be used to objectively measure joint angles and displacements (see figure 3.5).

Running technique is an important determinant of running economy, so by correcting faulty technique, running economy can be improved. Chapter 5 discusses running technique in greater detail.

ANTHROPOMETRIC MEASUREMENTS

Long-distance runners have among the lowest body fat mass in comparison to their respective peers from other sports. The average male and female has a body fat percentage of between 15 – 22 and 23 – 30 per cent respectively, whereas the average elite marathon runner has a percentage body fat of less than 10 per cent for male and less than 15 per cent for females.

Body composition can be measured in a number of ways. The more accurate methods, such as hydrostatic weighing and air displacement, are tedious and not often used apart from research purposes. Dual Energy X-ray Absorptiometry (DEXA) involves a 10 – 20 minute full body scan. It is safe, reliable, and relatively accurate, but somewhat costly.

A convenient and widely available method is Bioelectrical Impedance Analysis (BIA), where a mild, imperceptible current is passed through the body between a variable number of electrodes. Muscle will conduct the current easily while fat will impede it. The amount of electrical impedance gives an indirect indication of the amount of fat in the body. It provides quick estimates of the total fat mass, body fat percentage, lean body mass, and even basal metabolic rate. However, there are other variables that affect BIA, such as the level of hydration and intestinal contents that limit its accuracy. Generally, BIA is not recommended for serial monitoring of your body fat, as it is not accurate enough to detect week-to-week or month-to-month body fat changes.

An accurate yet practical method of assessing body fat would be the measurement of skinfolds. The double-layer thickness of the pinched up fold of skin is measured using a special caliper. Skinfolds are usually measured at different sites of the body to provide a better reflection of the overall body fat level. The sum-of-seven skinfolds, where the skinfolds at seven specified sites are added up to give a total in millimetres, is a good way of monitoring your body fat changes. Alternatively, the values of the skinfolds at the different sites are entered into an equation to derive the overall percentage of body fat, but this introduces error as the regression equations commonly used are derived from studies using Caucasian cadavers. It has been reported that the error for skinfold measurement to be between 3 – 5 per cent, so you will need to have your skinfolds measured by a trained individual in order to get consistent results.

Training for a marathon seems easy at first sight — keep increasing your mileage until you can cover 42 km at one go! However, I am sure that every runner has certain pre-requisites apart from completing the distance. For instance, finishing in one piece, within a certain training timeframe, achieving a particular finishing time, within a cap on the training hours that you are willing to commit per week, or achieving a certain rate of improvement. To fulfil these pre-requisites, one has to train smart, and train efficiently. In essence, to achieve maximum results with minimum effort, we need a training plan.

Even though the principles of training and exercise science are quite consistent, training programmes differ greatly between coaches. There is a multitude of training recommendations for the same objective, making it difficult for the runner to get a straight answer on how to train. The reasons for the varied recommendations are: (1) There is a lot of inter-individual variation in terms of runners' physiology and aptitude, so it is difficult to come out with a one-size-fits-all training programme; (2) Training can be prescribed accurately only if the runner's exercise testing results (e.g. $\dot{V}O_{2max}$, $v\dot{V}O_{2max}$, lactate threshold, running economy, gait analysis) are known, but the majority of runners do not have access to exercise testing; and (3) Coaches and runners often prefer to keep their training programmes a secret. Hence, the training of a runner is currently more an art than a science. To help navigate our way through this maze of training prescriptions, we shall describe the current consensus. To refine and optimise the training prescriptions further, you will have to depend on your feel. For example, we may prescribe a weekly long slow run of 25 – 35 km; exactly what mileage within that range is best for you will have to depend on your own feel or sense of what specific distance your body best responds well to.

TARGET SETTING

This book is targeted mainly at runners who have been running or jogging regularly for at least a year, and now wish to train more seriously and systematically for a marathon or half marathon. So if you are totally new to running, start running regularly first.

Aim to complete your first 10 km race, then move on to a 15 km race, then a half marathon, and finally a full marathon. It may be a good idea to do two to three half marathons before attempting the full, as the difficulty between a half and a full marathon is not double, but quadruple!

If you are not an experienced runner and are preparing for your first marathon, simply completing the race would be an achievement. Avoid aiming for a fast time on your first try. Give yourself at least six months to prepare for a marathon — nine to 12 months would be preferable. Many runners who have completed a half marathon expect to finish the full marathon in double the time, forgetting that the physiological requirements for running a marathon is very different from a half marathon or 10 km race. Unlike the latter races,

TIPS ON GETTING STARTED

Running is one of the simplest sports there is. All you need is a good pair of running shoes and light attire. You can do it anywhere, at any time. You can do it alone or with friends. To get started, remember:

- Have fun — find a pleasant park, enjoy the fresh air!
- Set realistic targets — aim to complete shorter distance races before going on to longer distances.
- Do not expect instant results. Running offers delayed gratification.
- Adopt the right mental attitude — who says feeling exhausted is bad? If you feel exhausted, then you know that you have put in a good effort and can give yourself a pat on the back.
- Running can be a social sport — use the opportunity to catch up with friends and family and chat while you jog. Join one of many running clubs in Singapore.
- Run on alternate days, so that there is plenty of time to recover before your next workout. Running two to three days a week is good for a start.
- If you are totally new to running, start by alternating between walking and jogging, e.g. walk 10 min, jog 5 min, and so on.
- In the early stages, set the time (e.g. exercise duration of 20 min) as your goal for each session. Do not worry about the distance or pace.
- Progressively increase the duration, until you can complete 30 min per session.
- Once you can do this, progressively shorten the walking duration while increasing the jogging duration (e.g. walk 10 min, jog 10 min; then walk 5, jog 10) until you are jogging continuously for 30 min.
- From here on, increase the duration or the frequency (i.e. number of training days per week) progressively.
- Listen to your body and pace yourself — what's the rush?
- Warm up and stretch before your run, and cool down and stretch after your run.
- Run tall (i.e. avoid hunching) and look up to see the world passing by as you run.

Ghana Segaran
Head, Panel of coaches for Middle and Long distance
Singapore Athletic Association

the amount of energy needed to complete a full marathon exceeds the energy within the carbohydrate stores. If you can complete the full marathon in double your half marathon time plus 10 min, you would have done extremely well.

For runners who have completed marathons, dramatic improvements are achievable in the first few marathons. But as you become faster, do not expect to shave huge chunks off your finishing time. For serious amateur runners, the magical number is the sub-3, i.e. completing the marathon in less than three hours. Many dream of doing a sub-3. Some will realize their dream, others will not. It is the journey that matters more.

The beauty of the marathon is that ultimately, you are racing against yourself — challenging your own limits. Each runner has a unique physiological makeup and external circumstance, so resist comparing against another runner and trying to beat his or her time. Instead, focus on making progress and achieving your own potential.

In your training diary, write down your motivation for doing the marathon, goals, current race or training timings, available training time (or the training time you are willing to commit), likes and dislikes, strengths, and weaknesses.

> "Nothing is sweeter than a journey made with friends. I couldn't have gotten back into shape within three months without friends and family support. Those long runs, chatting, and eating sessions after the runs — these I enjoyed, together with the commitment we had between us. The end result was secondary. On my fourth marathon, I had set a target of 3:05 to 3:10, but to achieve a sub-3 was a pleasant surprise! I am glad to have made it into the sub-3 club, together with four other runners at last year's Singapore Marathon, and I hope this will motivate more runners towards fulfilling their dream of bettering their times."
>
> — Sivakumar, who completed the 2008 Singapore Marathon in 2:59, placing him among the five Singapore men who completed the marathon in under three hours.

"I make it a point to plan for the long term, even a few years ahead, not just for the next race. From there, I set intermediate and near term goals, down to the goals for each training session to monitor my progression. My goals are slightly more challenging than my current form — they are realistic and attainable."

Daniel Ling, who finished the 2007 Singapore Marathon (local men's champion) in a personal best time of 2:46:31.

TRAINING GOALS

The whole idea behind training is to progressively induce training adaptations. Specifically, these include:

1. The ability of the muscles, tendons, and bones to tolerate repeated impact from running

2. Improving maximal aerobic capacity, or $\dot{V}O_{2max}$, by increasing the ability to transport and extract oxygen. This is achieved via increased plasma volume, increased stroke volume of the heart, increased red blood cells in the blood, increased capillarity surrounding the muscle fibres, and increased oxidative enzymes.

3. Increasing the lactate threshold (i.e. to be able to run faster without accumulating lactate in the blood)

4. Increasing speed

5. Increasing running economy

6. Increasing the carbohydrate stores

7. Improving the body's ability to mobilize fat faster during exercise

8. Acclimatization or ability to dissipate heat

9. Developing a sense of the race pace, to achieve accurate pacing during a race

TRAINING INTENSITY

The runner's training is described by its intensity and volume, i.e. how hard and how much he or she trains. Training intensity can be defined as a percentage of the maximum heart rate (HR_{max}), percentage of the $\dot{V}O_{2max}$, or running pace/speed.

HR_{max} Prescribing training intensity based on the HR_{max}, where HR_{max} = 220 – age, is the most convenient and is used the most often. For example, if you are 35 years old and wish to run at 70 per cent of your HR_{max}, then you should be maintaining a heart rate of 0.7 x (220 – 35) = 130 beats per minute. A variation of this is to use the heart rate reserve (HRR) instead of the HR_{max}, where HRR = HR_{max} – resting heart rate. Prescribing intensity as a percentage of HRR is more accurate and is gradually becoming more commonplace.

To measure your heart rate, place your fingers over your radial artery in the wrist or the carotid artery in the neck, and count the number of beats over 15 seconds, then multiply this by four to get the number of beats per minute. During training, you can stop for 15 seconds during your run to do this (for long runs), or you can measure it just after each work bout during interval training. A more convenient way is to wear a heart rate monitor.

It would be useful to get heart rate monitors that allow you to set upper and lower training heart rate limits, so that an alarm will alert you when you are running too fast or too slowly. When running on treadmills, you can use the built-in heart rate sensor available on most machines

$\dot{V}O_2max$ **or** $v\dot{V}O_2max$ Prescribing training intensity based on a percentage of your $\dot{V}O_2max$ is more precise, but you will first need to have your $\dot{V}O_2max$ measured. Indirect measurements of $\dot{V}O_2max$ (e.g. using software that come with some heart rate monitors, or using field tests) are generally not accurate enough, and you may be better off by simply setting your intensity based on your HR_{max}.

Running Pace Training intensity can also be based on the running pace, e.g. pace runs, where you run at your race speed. This can be in terms of kilometre per hour (km/h) or, more commonly minutes per kilometre (min/km). The latter is useful as there are often kilometre markers along the course of the marathon, and thinking in terms of min/km makes it easier to gauge if you are running according to your planned pace.

If you undergo a direct $\dot{V}O_2max$ measurement, you can obtain the speed at which the $\dot{V}O_2max$ was reached, i.e. $v\dot{V}O_2max$. Setting your training pace for the various types of training runs based on the $v\dot{V}O_2max$ is very precise, if you can have it measured.

TRAINING VOLUME

The training volume gives us an idea of the training stress, although it is not the only contributor. In order to monitor training efficiency and avoid overtraining and injuries, it is important to track your mileage per session and your weekly training mileage. For example, you may want to build up your long runs to 30 km per session and your weekly mileage to 60 km per week. When the term mileage is used, it usually means weekly mileage.

Alternatively, you could monitor the time spent running instead, e.g. a 40 minute easy run or a weekly training time of six hours. Tracking the training volume based on time is a good idea if you are new to distance running, as it gives a better estimate of training stress compared to mileage. A slower runner may take 80 minutes to run 10 km compared to 50 minutes for a faster runner, and therefore is subjected to more physical stress even though the distance run is the same.

TYPES OF TRAINING RUNS

A systematic and well-structured training plan or programme is necessary if you intend to step up your game and aim to complete the marathon in a certain time. The training plan comprises several types of training runs, each with its own objectives. If you wish to adopt a systematic approach to your training, the first and most critical step is to understand what each type of run is aimed at developing. Table 4.1 on page 61 summarizes the objectives (notations refer to the training adaptations numbered in the 'Training Goals' section; bold numbers denote primary focus) for each type of training run.

Base Run

These are easy pace, low-intensity (65 – 80 per cent of HR_{max}, corresponding to lactate threshold 1 or lower) runs that do not put a significant strain on the body. Lasting 30 – 60 minutes, these runs are usually used as 'fillers' in between other types of training to make up a targeted weekly mileage. For example, if you do a long run on Sunday, a track session (training on a running track) on Wednesday, and have two rest days, then the other three days of the week can be spent doing base runs.

Recovery runs, which are done the day after a hard workout or race, can be considered a base run — they are usually a very easy 20 – 30 minute run meant to reduce delayed onset muscle soreness (DOMS) and accelerate recovery.

At the start of your training cycle, when you do not want to load your body excessively, the bulk of your training days will be set aside for base runs. They are gentle on the body and are great for building foundation or maintaining fitness.

Despite the low intensity, base runs are effective in adapting the musculoskeletal system to the impact forces during running — even for a slow jog, the impact forces are two to three times bodyweight. For those with a low base, these runs can also improve the aerobic capacity. For very fit runners, base runs help to maintain aerobic fitness, and are therefore useful during the tapering phase just before a race. Another purpose of the base run is that it helps the body acclimatize to the heat, so when racing in a hotter climate, runners arrive several days earlier to do base runs to acclimatize to the heat.

Long Slow Run

To avoid stressing your body excessively and risking injuries, long runs are done at a slow pace (65 – 80 per cent of HR_{max}, or less than lactate threshold 1), well below the race pace. Like base runs, long slow runs help the musculoskeletal system adapt to the pounding while it increases aerobic capacity. Because of the much longer duration, long slow runs offer further benefits, the most significant of which is to induce changes in the body's biochemistry — they expand the carbohydrate stores and train the body to mobilize fat faster. These adaptations tune our energy stores to fuel our muscles for long exercise bouts such as the marathon. To optimise such adaptations, the long run has to extend beyond the point where the runner

Table 4.1 Types of Training Runs

Training Run	Objectives#	Intensity (% HR$_{max}$*)	Description
Base Run	❶❷❽	65 – 80	Easy runs lasting 30 – 60 min or 6 – 12 km
Long Slow Run	❶❷❻❼❽	65 – 80	Easy runs of 60 – 180 min or 12 – 38 km
Pace Run	❶❷❸❺❻❼❾	80 – 90	Steady runs at race pace for up to 90 min or 25 km
Tempo Run	❶❷❸❹❺	88 – 92	Comfortably hard runs of 20 – 60 min or 5 – 10 km
Aerobic Intervals	❶❷❹❺	95 – 100	Repeated runs of 3 – 5 min or 800 – 1,200 m each, at a work:rest ratio of 1:1
Speed Intervals	❶❸❹❺	100	Repeats of 200 – 600 m with full recoveries in between
Hill Training	❶❷❸❹❺	100	Any of the above runs on hilly terrain
Fartlek	❶❷❸❹❺	Variable	Free form running in various training zones and gradients

\#   Numbers in bold denote primary focus
*   HR$_{max}$: Maximum heart rate, taken as 220 – age

❶ Increasing the ability of the muscles, tendons, and bones to tolerate repeated impact from running.

❷ Improving maximal aerobic capacity, or VO$_2$max, by increasing the ability to transport and extract oxygen. This is achieved via increased plasma volume, increased stroke volume of the heart, increased red blood cells in the blood, increased capillarity surrounding the muscle fibres, and increased oxidative enzymes.

❸ Increasing the lactate threshold (i.e. to be able to run faster without accumulating lactate in the blood).

❹ Increasing speed.

❺ Increasing running economy.

❻ Increasing the carbohydrate stores.

❼ Improving the body's ability to mobilize fat faster during exercise.

❽ Acclimatization or ability to dissipate heat.

❾ Developing a sense of the race pace, to achieve accurate pacing during a race.

usually 'hits the wall,' i.e. when the carbohydrate stores run out, forcing the body to mobilise the body fat. That is why long slow runs stretch anywhere from 20 km to 38 km. Another purpose of the long slow run is to build confidence — if you can comfortably run 38 km at one go during training, then you can tell yourself that for the actual race, you need to cover only 4 km more.

If you are unable to run 20 km at one go, start with what you can (e.g. 12 km) and build up from there. As you progressively lengthen your long slow runs to two hours, be wary of overuse injuries.

There are runners who do 'over-distance' training, where they go beyond 42 km for their long runs, so that the actual marathon distance becomes a cinch for them. Such runners are extremely experienced and fit, so they need to push beyond the usual in order to induce further adaptations. For the majority of runners, long runs building up to 30 – 35 km would suffice, and going beyond 38 km may be counterproductive, meaning that their injuries would outweigh any fitness gains they might make.

The vast majority of runners do only one long run per week, usually on the weekends. Some may do a mid-week long run in addition, but usually these are about ¾ the distance or duration of the weekend long run. The long runs should comprise 25 – 30 per cent of the weekly mileage.

Pace Run

Pacing is critical during an endurance race — there is an optimal pace that will help you achieve your personal best time. Most of us will estimate what this pace is based on our previous race times and how we felt during the race. For example, if you finished your last marathon very comfortably in four hours flat (i.e. 5:40 min/km or 10.5 km/h), then you may wish to plan a race pace of 5:20 min/km or 11.3 km/h to finish the marathon in 3 hr 45 min. The race pace usually works out to between 90 per cent of HR_{max} for fast runners and 88 per cent of HR_{max} for slower runners. Typically, pace runs are less than 90 min or less than 25 km.

If you have completed half marathons and are aiming to compete in your first marathon, then a rough rule of thumb is to aim to finish in double your half marathon time plus 10 minutes. For example, if you completed your last half marathon in two hours flat (i.e. 5:43 min/km), then aim for a race pace of 5:55 min/km to finish the marathon in 4 hr 10 min. A more conservative projection by Paul Tergat, former marathon world record holder with a time of 2:04:55, estimates the marathon pace by adding 10 per cent to the half marathon pace, e.g. if your half marathon time is 2 hours flat, then your marathon pace should be 10 per cent slower than 5:43 min, or 6:17 min/km to finish in 4 hr 25 min.

Most runners adopt the strategy of holding an even race pace throughout the entire race. The pace run serves to get the runner accustomed to running at race pace. The runner should acquire a good sense of the race pace so that he or she can maintain that pace during the race, regardless of the conditions. Often large crowds, weather conditions, the pace of fellow runners around us, fatigue, and inaccurate distance markers throw us off our intended pace during the race and derail our chances of finishing within our targeted time. Pace runs are also used to simulate race conditions and used as opportunities to practice taking in water and energy gels.

Tempo Run

Tempo runs are sustained, 'comfortably hard' runs at a steady pace for 5 – 10 km. Lactic acid (lactate) builds up in the blood as running speed increases. Above a certain speed, the lactate is unable to maintain a steady state (meaning that the body is unable to get rid of lactate at the same rate that it is produced) and accumulates rapidly, to the point where it is impossible to continue running (see figure 3.3, page 49). This point is called the onset of blood lactate accumulation (OBLA, or lactate threshold 2). The tempo run is a threshold run, whereby the running speed is at or slightly above the OBLA. Hence, they can be sustained for a limited period only.

Tempo runs are primarily aimed at taxing the anaerobic system and training the body to clear lactate quickly. As the body adapts to this, the lactate threshold increases such that the runner can sustain higher running speeds for the same running duration. Tempo runs also offer a psychological effect — it trains the runner to endure the fatigue from the lactate build-up. Hence, tempo runs are one of the most productive types of run for distance runners.

Your OBLA — and the corresponding running speed at the OBLA — can be measured by doing a lactate profile in the laboratory (see page 49 – 50). But if you do not have access to lactate profiling, the alternative is to use your 10 km race pace, as this approximates your running speed at OBLA. If you have never done a 10 km race, then do a time trial.

To do a tempo run, start with shorter distances, such as 3 km. Cover that distance at your 10 km race pace, holding a steady pace throughout. Do not start out too fast, or you will not be able to sustain the pace all the way to the end. Every two or more weeks, progressively increase the tempo run distance, such that you have to hold your 10 km race pace for longer and longer. If you can progressively lengthen your tempo runs to 10 km, then that would suffice for most competitive runners. Stronger runners can go up to 15 km for their tempo runs.

In the build-up before the marathon, sign up for races of shorter distances, such as 5, 10, and 15 km races, and consider them as your 'tempo runs' (they are actually faster than your tempo runs). They serve as a good gauge of your progress and can be good predictors of your marathon performance. For example, if you can do a sub-40 minute for a 10 km race, then you know you've got a crack at doing a sub-3 hr marathon. For a sub-4 hr marathon, you will need to be able to run 10 km in under 52 minutes.

Tempo runs are very taxing, especially the longer ones. To reduce the stress, an alternative form of threshold training called cruise intervals is often used. Cruise intervals are run at the same speed as the threshold run, except that brief rest intervals are introduced to break up the run. For example, the cruise interval equivalent of a 10 km tempo run could be a 2 km run at the same pace as the 10 km tempo run, followed by a one minute recovery, followed by a 2 km run and so on, i.e. five repeats of 2 km run with rest intervals of one minute. Each work bout of the cruise interval should vary between three and 15 minutes. The rest interval should not be more than two minutes, as you do not want the blood lactate to fall too much. Cruise intervals help in enhancing lactate clearance.

> "The most important attribute in a distance runner is stamina — the ability to run long and hard. There are a few different workouts that can build stamina, and if you were to ask me to choose only one, I would choose to do tempo runs."
>
> – Murugiah Rameshon,
> Holder of Singapore's national marathon record time of 2:24:22

Aerobic Intervals

The faster we run, the more we tax our aerobic system, until we reach maximal aerobic capacity, or $\dot{V}O_2max$. The speed at which we achieve $\dot{V}O_2max$ is the $v\dot{V}O_2max$, and this pace is higher than that of OBLA and corresponds to close to 100 per cent of HR_{max}. If we were to run continuously at $v\dot{V}O_2max$, the pace would be too taxing to sustain for significant durations. By doing repeated bouts of running at $v\dot{V}O_2max$, we accumulate time at maximal aerobic capacity, thereby improving aerobic capacity. Hence, the name aerobic intervals. A 1 per cent improvement in maximal aerobic capacity translates to a 1 per cent increase in race speed.

When we start running at a hard pace, it takes about two minutes for the aerobic system to ramp up to its maximal capacity. That is why the work bouts in aerobic intervals are at least two minutes, usually a minimum of three minutes. If we sustain $v\dot{V}O_2max$ for more than five minutes, the blood lactate builds up to significant levels, forcing the runner to slow down below $v\dot{V}O_2max$. Hence, work bouts in aerobic interval training are typically three to five minutes or approximately 800 – 1,200 m. Most coaches and runners prefer a work bout of five minutes (i.e. 1,000 – 1,200 m repeats), as this gives them more time at maximal aerobic capacity — in this case, as it takes two minutes to ramp up to maximal aerobic capacity, the runner would spend three minutes at maximal aerobic capacity for each work bout. The rest intervals should be long enough to allow the runner to push to $v\dot{V}O_{2max}$ for the next bout of running, and this usually means a work:rest ratio of 1:1. Each running bout will be a comfortably hard run, at or very close to your maximal heart rate (or at $v\dot{V}O_{2max}$ if you have had it measured). For example, you could do four to 10 repeats of 1,000 m. If you take four minutes to complete each 1,000 m, then your rest interval between each run should be four minutes. As standard distances are usually used for aerobic interval training, the training is usually done on a running track. Aim for an even pace, and even timings for each repeat. Avoid pushing too hard for the first few repeats as that will lead to a suboptimal pace for subsequent repeats.

> "Interval training is definitely the main contributor towards my personal best. It is my key to running faster and further. Initially, running long distances at a constant pace helped me improve. But after running for a year or two, it didn't help that much anymore. The rest and burst alternations of interval training, although brutally painful, has helped me break through the three-hour barrier."
>
> – Kumaravel, whose Singapore Marathon times between 2006 to 2008 were 3:28:17, 3:12:39, and 2:58:13. Two months after going sub-3 in Singapore, he recorded a 2:51:40 in the 2009 Hong Kong Marathon.

Speed Intervals

While the aerobic intervals are designed to enhance aerobic capacity, speed intervals are aimed at improving speed and running economy. As the training intensity is high, the work bouts tend to be short, typically 200 – 600 m. The pace for each bout of running should be significantly above race pace, with the heart rate hitting HR_{max}. The actual pace depends on what you are training for — it is faster for 10,000 m runners than it is for marathon runners. For marathoners, it should not be an all-out sprint, as the running technique during a sprint differs somewhat from the fast cruising speed that the marathoner should be practicing.

For such short and intense bouts, the anaerobic system comes into play, with minimal involvement of the aerobic system (remember, it takes two minutes to ramp up to maximal aerobic capacity). Importantly, by running at an almost all-out pace over 200 – 600 m, the high impact forces strengthen the muscles, thereby improving running speed. I consider this a form of strength training that is specific to running. In typical resistance training (weight training) in the gym, the speed of muscle contraction (e.g. when doing leg presses) does not approximate to that of running. Furthermore, running involves eccentric muscle action, whereby the muscles attempt to contract while it is being lengthened due to the momentum of the limbs. An example of this is the hamstring muscles, which are lengthened as the lower limb swings forward, but at the same time, the body contracts the hamstrings to decelerate the limb. Such eccentric action exerts a heavy toll on the hamstrings, resulting in tears. With typical resistance training, it is difficult to train the muscles eccentrically to help them tolerate the eccentric loading encountered during running. This is where speed training provides the eccentric loading and specificity.

Speed training also improves neuromuscular coordination, so that over time the runner is able to maintain the same fast pace while looking smoother and more relaxed. The strength and neuromuscular adaptations both contribute to running economy, an important determinant of performance in distance runners. With a higher running economy, the runner is able to run at a faster pace while consuming less oxygen and therefore less energy.

As it is important to maintain a fast pace during speed training, the rest interval should be long enough such that a good effort can be made, with a good running form, for the next running bout. Typically, the work:rest ratio is 1:2 to 1:4. During the rest interval, it is up to the runner whether to do a slow run, walk, or stretch — whichever makes the runner feel rested enough to put in a good effort in the next running bout. The total distance covered should not exceed 8 km. Resist running too fast for the first few repeats, e.g. if you are doing 10 repeats of 400 m, aim to complete each of the 400 m in similar timings rather than fading towards the end. Like aerobic intervals, speed intervals are usually done on a running track so that the running distances can be determined accurately.

Technique is key during speed training, even for marathoners. Poor technique may get reinforced during speed training and should be corrected. To maintain good running form during speed interval training, observe the following pointers:

- Eyes focused at the end of the lane — tunnel vision
- Head in line with the spine — held high and square
- Chin down (rather than up)
- Shoulders held down, back, relaxed, and square to the lane

- Smooth forward and backward action of the arms (avoid going across the body), brushing the vest, and driving the elbows far back. The hands should swing from shoulder height to the hips for men; from bust height to the hips for women

- Elbows flexed at 90° throughout

- Hands relaxed, fingers loosely curled, thumb uppermost

- The trunk stabilises the whole running movement — observe centering, breathing, and a neutral spine (see core strengthening, pages 159 – 172). Lean slightly forward but not bent over

- Bring the knees high up at the end of the forward swing. Rotate the hip forward with the forward swing of the lower limb to help extend the stride

- Bring the foot down in a claw action. Heel-, midfoot-, or forefoot-strike are all acceptable, as long as the foot lands under your centre of gravity and you achieve a good rebound

- Fully extend the knee of the rear leg during toe off

- Stand tall, stay relaxed and smooth, while ensuring maximum drive

The speed technique described above consumes a lot of energy, so it should be used for short spells only, such as clearing the starting line, overtaking, and finishing. When cruising, use the technique described in Chapter 5.

Hill Training

By doing your base run, long slow run, pace run, or tempo run over a hilly terrain, or performing your aerobic intervals or speed intervals over an upslope, you can raise the loading on your muscles up a notch. It is a form of resistance training for runners, as the runner works against the resistance of the slope. Hill workouts develop greater power and strength, which in turn improves running economy. Hill training can also improve running technique as it encourages the runner to lean forward, drive the elbows back, and lift the knees higher. A word of caution: You will need to have a very firm foundation before attempting hill workouts.

Running downhill develops speed and acceleration, but is associated with much higher impact forces and eccentric muscle activity. Runners participating in the Boston Marathon often complain of excessive hamstring soreness because of the long downhill stretches along parts of the course. So if you are running cross-country or over a hilly terrain, attack the upslopes, but go easy when running downhill. If the marathon you are preparing for happens to be a hilly one, then it pays to include hill training in your training programme.

Fartlek

A Swedish term meaning "speed play," fartlek is a free-form workout comprising a variable mix of runs at variable paces from easy pace to race pace, threshold pace, or even speed interval pace, all combined into one training session. An example would be going for a run in a relatively hilly or cross-country terrain, and sprinting up alternate hills — the intensity varies according to the gradient and length of the slopes you are presented with. The sudden change in pace allows the body to practice changing from one running mode/pace to another, and breaks the monotony of the training session.

For recommendations on venues in Singapore for the various types of training runs, refer to appendix 2.

RUNNING DRILLS

Running drills help improve our movement patterns. Often, certain movements are exaggerated in such drills to help acquire a certain habit (e.g. knee lifts), activate specific muscles (e.g. hamstrings), and work secondary muscles to achieve better muscle balance (e.g. side strides crossover). These drills are demonstrated in the following pages.

These drills are usually practiced before a training session, in order to fire the muscles up and get the body into a better running form for the subsequent workout. They should certainly be done before an intensive workout, such as aerobic or speed intervals, but can also be done before all training sessions. Do them at least once a week.

Before doing the drills, warm up with a slow five to 10 minute easy run, followed by stretches. Over a straight 50 m stretch that is either flat or slightly uphill, do the drills in the following sequence, jogging slowly back to the starting point to commence the next drill.

(1) PUSH OFF

Aim: To activate calf muscles for toe-off
Action: While running, push off maximally

(2) BUTT KICKS

Aim: To activate the hamstrings

Action: As above, plus bring the back of your
heels towards the buttocks

(3) KNEE LIFTS (SKIPPING)

Aim: To activate the hip flexors and promote a
high knee lift and therefore better foot strike

Action: As above, plus lift the knees high enough
such that at the end of the forward
swing, your thighs are parallel to the
ground, lower leg vertical and ankles
dorsiflexed

(4) CLAW BACK

Aim: To activate the hamstrings further

Action: As above, but extend the knee during the
forward swing and pull the foot back
before it strikes the ground

(5) SIDE CROSSOVER

Aim: To activate the hip adductors and abductors, and the trunk rotators

Action: While jogging sideways on the balls of your feet towards your right, bring your left foot across the front of your right leg; then take a step towards your right with your right foot then cross your left foot behind your right leg to take another step to your right, and repeat this sequence. Do one repeat to your right and the next one to your left.

(6) JUMPING STRIDES

Aim: To activate all the running muscles

Action: Stride forward, aiming to stride longer and higher, while bringing the thighs up to the horizontal

(7) ACCELERATION

Aim: To activate all the running muscles in a
        more natural gait

Action: To finish off, accelerate gradually over
        the 50 m stretch

PERIODIZATION

What happens if we adopt a changeless training program? In response to a constant training load, the body initially enters the shock phase where the runner experiences a drop in performance. After a short period, the body goes into the supercompensation phase, where adaptation to the training load occurs, accompanied by improved performance. The adaptations will soon plateau. Unless the training load changes, the body next enters the maladaptation phase where problems like overtraining, overuse injuries, and chronic fatigue plague the runner.

Benefits of Varying Your Training Intensity and Volume

To avoid the maladaptation phase, it pays to vary the training intensity and volume (mileage), and divide the whole training program into cycles, phases, and periods. Hence, the term periodization (cyclical training). Within each training cycle, the training intensity and volume are altered progressively. This benefits the runner in a number of ways:

- A runner's form undulates in a cyclical manner. There will be good weeks (when you feel energetic and are recording good training times) and not-so-good weeks — it is impossible to be in top form all the time. Periodization serves to modify the training intensity and volume such that they conform to the runner's innate cycle. Hence the training is light during a period when the runner is at risk of fatigue; training is heavy when the runner is fresh; and training tapers off to allow the runner to recover in time for a major competition.

- The high volume and low intensity typically used at the beginning of each cycle contributes to the success of the periodized model because it beneficially alters body composition and prepares the runner to better tolerate the higher intensities later in the cycle.

- The low volume, high intensity phase towards the end of the cycle reduces the risk of overtraining.

- The variations within the course of each cycle prevent staleness. Varying the volume and intensity forces the neuromuscular system to continuously adapt to the training load.

How Do I Periodize My Training?

Designing a periodized training program requires experience, through trial and error. It is more an art than a science. Put simply, the steps are:

1. Decide the race or races you wish to peak for. You can have one or two major peaks in a year, and a couple of minor peaks. Typically, marathon runners peak for one or two marathons a year. The period from the commencement of your training till just after your last major event forms a macrocycle, and this usually stretches over a year.

2. Divide your macrocycle into mesocycles, with each mesocycle preferably culminating in a minor peak (e.g. for a 10 km or half marathon race). Each mesocycle should be approximately two to three months long, so the number of mesocycles you have within each macrocycle will depend on the length of your macrocycle. Each mesocycle builds upon the previous one, so the runner gets progressively stronger.

3. Divide each mesocycle into a preparatory, competition, and transition period. Of course, the major competitions should fall within the competition period (pre-season and in-season). You can have minor, unimportant events during the preparatory period (off-season). There should be no events during the transition period (immediate post competition period).

4. Start with a comfortable mileage (e.g. half of your peak mileage) during the preparatory period and quickly build up to a high mileage but low intensity. The intensity is progressively increased (e.g. addition of high pace runs, tempo runs, interval training, hill training, etc.) while the mileage is reciprocally cut back a little. The preparatory period is further divided into the first endurance phase (endurance-1), strength phase, speed phase, second endurance (endurance-2) phase, and taper phase (see figure 4.1 page 74).

   Endurance-1 starts with base runs and long slow runs to accumulate mileage, which in turn reduces excess body fat, increases aerobic base, and conditions the musculoskeletal system for higher intensity training later. The duration of endurance-1 varies, depending on the how long you have been running. An experience runner will have a strong base, so the mileage can be stepped up quickly. Newer runners will have to build up mileage gradually, say by 10 per cent per week.

   During the **strength** phase, pace runs, tempo runs, aerobic intervals, and fartlek training are introduced into the programme. Which kind of workout the runner employs depends on his needs. Usually, one or two of the above workouts are performed per week (certainly not all of them). As these workouts are intensive, it is difficult to tolerate more than two sessions per week. Beginners (e.g. in the first year of training) may even wish to forgo such workouts altogether, and only include them in the next macrocycle.

During the **speed** phase, speed intervals and/or hill training are added to the weekly programme to bring the intensity up a notch. Again, this depends on whether the runner can tolerate such intensive workouts. Newer runners may want to avoid them and only do such workouts in their third or subsequent macrocycles.

Endurance-2 represents the final mileage build-up leading to the big race. The mileage is stepped up while the intensity is reduced to condition the body for the gruelling marathon. For example, the long slow runs progress to 35 km per run while the intensive workouts are limited to once a week or once every two weeks. Fewer repeats are done for interval training, while tempo run distances are reduced.

Finally, comes the **taper**, where the intensity is kept high while the mileage is drastically reduced (e.g. halved) to allow the body to recover and recharge. Do not try anything that is faster than what you have done previously. In other words, the taper phase is not the time to set personal best training times, although it is tempting to. The taper can last five to 14 days, depending on the individual's mileage and recovery rate. The higher the mileage and the slower the recovery rate, the longer the taper. Too long a taper and the body de-conditions; too short and the body is not fully recharged for the marathon.

5. In most sports, the **competition** period can last months (e.g. soccer season where a match is played every week for months) whereas for marathoners it is very short, as distance runners cannot pack in many distance races in the space of a few months. As mentioned earlier, the usual recommendation is to do a marathon race once every six months. Hence, the competition period for marathon runners typically comprise a tune-up, shorter distance race (e.g. 10 km or half marathon) and the marathon itself a few weeks later.

6. During the one to four week **transition** period, runners take a total break away from running to recuperate from the stresses sustained over 42 km of pounding. During this time, runners are encouraged to participate non-impact recreational sports instead (active rest).

7. The **microcycle** is usually synonymous with the week's training programme, where there are variations in intensity and mileage from day to day. (More on the microcycle below.)

As an example, if you started training in March and were aiming to do the year-end Singapore Marathon, you could plan a nine-month macrocycle to peak in time for the race. Within these nine months, you could incorporate three three-month mesocycles. Pick races that coincide with the end of each macrocycle. Hence, the first macrocycle (March – May) could peak at the 15-km Passion Run held at the end of May. The second macrocycle (June – August) could peak at the Army Half Marathon in August. The final macrocycle (September – November) could peak at the Singapore Marathon in the first week of December.

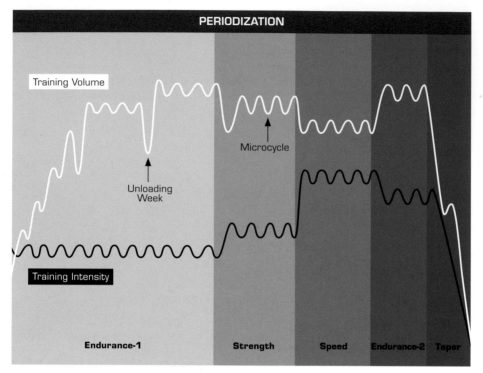

Figure 4.1. Illustration of a mesocycle. Each week is a microcycle. In this example, after every three weeks, there is an unloading week where the mileage is reduced to minimize the risk of overuse injuries.

PUTTING IT ALL TOGETHER

Now that you are familiar with the various types of training runs and understand periodization, we can start to structure each week's training. The week constitutes a single microcycle. Structure your weekly training programme by: (1) Deciding on the number of rest days you need; (2) Allocating the various types of training runs to each training day; (3) Planning the distance for each run to achieve a targeted weekly mileage and finally; (4) Periodizing.

Rest Days

After each bout of exercise, the body adapts to the training stimulus and overshoots the baseline (supercompenstation) (see figure 4.2). However, the supercompensation abates and returns to the baseline within four days. If the next training bout occurs more than four days after the previous one, then the runner's fitness will hover around the baseline in the long term. However, if the next training bout occurs before the adaptation returns to the baseline, then the runner is able to build on the previous adaptation and progressively increase his level of fitness (see figure 4.3). This is why training has to be regular, and anything less than three times a week is unlikely to lead to significant gains in fitness.

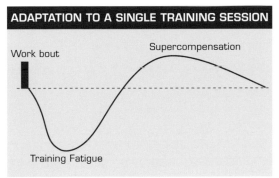

ADAPTATION TO A SINGLE TRAINING SESSION

Work bout

Supercompensation

Training Fatigue

ADAPTATION TO MULTIPLE TRAINING SESSIONS

Increasing Fitness

Figure 4.2. Adaptation following a single bout of exercise.

Figure 4.3. With regular training, the runner builds on the adaptation from the previous training session and progressively becomes fitter.

Elite runners have a very high fitness base, so the challenge for them is to provide adequate training stimulus or stress to elicit fitness increments. An elite runner who logs a weekly mileage of 200 km would lose his fitness even if he were to run 100 km a week! Recreational runners, on the other hand, will find it easy to stress the body to induce adaptations. In some cases, the challenge is in recovering fast enough.

If starting from a low base (e.g. if you have not been running previously), begin by running three times a week. If you already have a base, five to six days of training a week would ensure a good balance between stress and recovery. Very fit runners may train seven days a week, or even have two sessions per day.

If you have two or more rest days a week, it would be a good idea to spread them out, rather than have consecutive rest days. Here, rest days refer to days when you do not run — it does not necessarily mean that you do not exercise at all. You can spend your rest day(s) doing resistance training, core strengthening, non-impact sports, or stretches. This is referred to as "active rest."

"Listen to your body, don't be obsessed with numbers. Value quality over quantity, especially when time is not on your side. And remember, rest is a training session in itself — it's when the body recovers and gets stronger. I learned this the hard way. I had to take a year off racing in 2005 due to burn out."

– Jeanette Wang, two-time Sundown Ultramarathon (84 km) champion and one of Singapore's top Ironman.

Training Runs

Assuming you decided on having two rest days, then you would have five training days. How should you fill these five days with the different types of training runs discussed? It depends on how much training stress you wish to impose on your body, and what your weaknesses are.

For starters, you will definitely need to include a long slow run, since you are preparing for a distance event. This is usually done on during the weekend, as it takes up the most time.

Next, you can designate zero to two intensive workout days, depending on your 'training age' and fitness base. Training age refers to the number of years you have been running regularly, e.g. if you have been running for two years, then your training age is two years. A runner with a training age of less than a year can exclude intensive workout days from his or her programme. Specifically which type of training run you do on your intensive workout day depends on how much you wish to stress your body and what your weaknesses are, be it low aerobic capacity, low lactate threshold, poor speed, or poor running economy. Such assessments can be done through laboratory and field tests. If unsure, start with the least stressful (i.e. least intensive workout) and move upwards. In approximate order of increasing intensity, the workouts to choose from are pace runs, tempo runs, aerobic intervals, speed intervals, fartlek, and hill training (see table 4.1, page 61).

Which is more important: long slow runs or intensive workouts? For beginners, as mentioned earlier, intensive workouts are unnecessary as you can make significant gains without them. For intermediate and advanced distance runners, both are important — long slow runs, together with base runs, clock mileage to give the runner a good foundation upon which the intensive workouts are conducted; the intensive workouts give the runner the strength, running economy, and endurance to tolerate the long runs comfortably.

After setting aside rest days, long slow run days, and intensive workout days, fill the rest of the days of the week with base runs. Here is an example of what a typical weekly programme or microcycle looks like:

Monday	Tuesday	Wednesday	Thursday	Friday	Saturday	Sunday
Rest	Base Run	Base Run	Intensive Workout*	Rest	Base Run	Long Slow Run

* Intensive workout can be a pace run, tempo run, aerobic intervals, or speed intervals, fartlek, or hill training

Weekly Mileage

Next, decide what your weekly mileage will be. This could vary from 20 – 120 km, depending your training age. As a guide, your weekly mileage should approximate twice the race distance that you are training for. For example, if you are planning to do a 15 km race, then you need to build up to a mileage of 30 km per week. Likewise, a weekly mileage of 40 km is preferable to prepare for a half marathon; 80 km for a full marathon. If you are training for your first marathon or if your training age is less than two years, it is unlikely that you will be able to tolerate 80 km per week, so build up to 60 km per week instead.

Sub-3 marathon runners typically average 80 –120 km per week. The top runners in Singapore go up to 160 –190 km per week. World class, elite marathoners often exceed 200 km per week. Kenyan runner Paul Tergat, the former marathon world record holder (2:04:55, Berlin 2003) covers 260 – 280 km per week, and has weeks that almost hit 300 km. While individual tolerance varies, few will be able to clock such mileages without injury — run according to your own ability and listen to your own body.

Allocate the distance for each training run such that they add up to the targeted weekly mileage. Below is a training log showing the planned training distance for each day's run, totalling 40 km for the week. The empty cells are for the runner to fill in the actual distance run, run time, and pace.

MESOCYCLE 1	Mon	Tue	Wed	Thu	Fri	Sat	Sun	Week
Training	Rest	Base	Base	Workout	Rest	Base	LSD	Total
Date	1 Jan	2 Jan	3 Jan	4 Jan	5 Jan	6 Jan	7 Jan	1
Target (km)	0	6.0	6.0	5.0	0	5.0	18.0	40.0
Distance (km)								
Time (min)								
Pace (min/km)								
Remarks	Weights		Pace Run		Swim			

Periodization

To periodize the training, plan the mileages for the weeks ahead such that the mileage progresses in a cyclical manner. There are two common ways to do this: In block training cycles, the mileage remains the same for three weeks, followed by an unloading week where the training is lighter. The unloading week is where the mileage is intentionally low, to reduce the risk of overuse injuries and overtraining. The alternative is to have three incremental weeks followed by an unloading week (see figure 4.4).

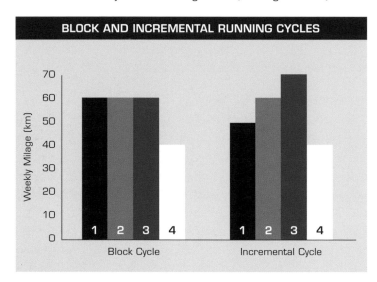

Figure 4.4. Two different types of four-week cycles. In the block cycle, the mileages are fixed for the first three weeks, whereas in the incremental cycle, they increase each week. For both cycles, the fourth week is an unloading week.

Whatever event I'm training for, be it a triathlon or running race, I base my programme on four-week blocks. That is, three weeks build up, one week easy. Each block gets harder than the one before, until it's time to taper. Over the years I've found this method to work best for me. Periodization is about training smart and knowing when to go hard and go easy."

— Jeanette Wang, two-time Sundown Ultramarathon champion and one of Singapore's top Ironman.

For each block of four weeks, the average mileage can be higher than the previous block, so that the mileage increases progressively. The example below demonstrates an incremental cycle where the targeted or planned mileage increases from 40 km to 45 km to 50 km, and then drops back to 40 km:

MESOCYCLE 1	Mon	Tue	Wed	Thu	Fri	Sat	Sun	Week
Training	**Rest**	**Base**	**Base**	**Workout**	**Rest**	**Base**	**LSD**	**Total**
Date	1 Jan	2 Jan	3 Jan	4 Jan	5 Jan	6 Jan	7 Jan	1
Target (km)	0	6.0	6.0	5.0	0	5.0	18.0	40.0
Distance (km)								
Time (min)								
Pace (min/km)								
Remarks	Weights		Pace Run	Tempo Run	Swim			
Date	8 Jan	9 Jan	10 Jan	11 Jan	12 Jan	13 Jan	14 Jan	2
Target (km)	0	7.0	7.0	5.0	0	6.0	20.0	45.0
Distance (km)								
Time (min)								
Pace (km/h)								
Remarks	Weights		Pace Run	Tempo Run	Swim			
Date	15 Jan	16 Jan	17 Jan	18 Jan	19 Jan	20 Jan	21 Jan	3
Target (km)	0	8.0	8.0	5.0	0	7.0	22.0	50.0
Distance (km)								
Time (min)								
Pace (min/km)								
Remarks	Weights		Pace Run	Tempo Run	Swim			
Date	22 Jan	23 Jan	24 Jan	25 Jan	26 Jan	27 Jan	28 Jan	4
Target (km)	0	6.0	6.0	5.0	0	5.0	18.0	40.0
Distance (km)								
Time (min)								
Pace (km/h)								
Remarks	Weights		Pace Run	Tempo Run	Swim			

TRAINING LOGS

It is a good idea not only to plan your training, but also to keep a log of your training. Training logs are especially useful when you wish to analyse the efficacy of your training. For example, if you were to acquire a stress fracture, you could go back to your training log to see what your training programme was like prior to the onset of symptoms. If your weekly mileage was, say 60 km in the weeks leading up to the onset of the stress fracture, then that could be considered your 'fracture threshold.' When you resume training after the injury and start building up your mileage, you would want to stay just below the fracture threshold for a longer duration to give your bones more time to adapt to the impact forces.

Or, if you found that your race times have been pretty good, you could refer back to your training log to see what you were doing right.

"Understanding my training patterns allows me to exploit and further develop my strengths and at the same time focus on improving my weaknesses. This is where a training log comes in extremely handy. My training log allows me to reflect, analyse and plan my training."

– Kumaravel, with a marathon personal best of 2:51:40 recorded at the 2009 Hong Kong Marathon.

A blank training log is provided in appendix 1 for your convenience. Make copies for use, or convert it to an Excel file so the weekly mileages can be computed in the right hand column for your convenience. An Excel training log can also be downloaded at www.myhealth.sg.

STICKING TO THE PLAN

Now that you can draw up a comprehensive training plan, the next step is to execute it. Marathon training requires discipline and consistency. No one ever said that training for a marathon was easy, and many are attracted to the marathon precisely because it is a challenge.

There are many excuses for skipping the training session — too busy, soreness, can't wake up, working late, and working shifts just to name a few. "No time" is the most common excuse. After encountering so many marathoners and triathletes in the course of my work, I noticed that it is the busiest of executives that take up the most time-consuming of sports. I have since come to the conclusion that such busy individuals are drawn to marathons and triathlons for three reasons. Firstly, these individuals are high-achievers, and non-competitive recreational activities such as shopping or having a leisurely lunch simply does not appeal to their competitive streaks. Secondly, marathon and triathlon training represent a form of "escape" from their busy and stressful work. The more time-consuming the sport, the longer they can "evade" their work. Of course, they do not see it as evasion, but rather as in investment in their competitiveness and health. Finally, and most importantly, their hectic schedules tend to turn their lives upside down, so they need an anchor in their lives. The training schedule, with its fixed routines serves as the anchor, and they work their schedules around this fixed anchor. By doing this, they achieve a sense of stability and regularity in their lives and end up being more productive.

Many assume that because marathon training is time-consuming and tiring, it reduces work productivity. On the contrary, marathon training increases work productivity. The training schedule forces the runner to have regular sleeping routines, which improves sleep quality — the runner sleeps soundly and wakes up more refreshed and ready to work, even if he has to wake up an hour earlier. Exercise also increases alertness, again contributing to work productivity. Running also reduces stress, and we work more effectively when we are not overly stressed. Often, you hear of people who report that they are cranky without their exercise. Others will say that they cannot function at work without first going for their exercise session.

To overcome the excuses or hurdles to exercising, draw up your training plan and stick to it. Choose a running time that you have full control of, e.g. early in the morning, so that if you miss the session, you have no one else to blame but yourself. Next, recognise that there is a 'speed bump' whenever you commence an exercise programme — in the initial stages, it will be tiring and you have to drag yourself through it. But as you get fitter and get to the other side of the bump, it becomes easier and easier. When I first started running, a 6 km run was a chore; now a routine weekday 16 km base run feels refreshing. There are slopes along my regular jogging route that I had to walk up, and how I used to dread those hills. Now, I cross those hills without having to slow down and often, I am not even conscious of the inclines.

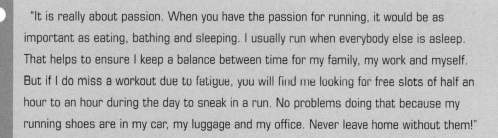

"It is really about passion. When you have the passion for running, it would be as important as eating, bathing and sleeping. I usually run when everybody else is asleep. That helps to ensure I keep a balance between time for my family, my work and myself. But if I do miss a workout due to fatigue, you will find me looking for free slots of half an hour to an hour during the day to sneak in a run. No problems doing that because my running shoes are in my car, my luggage and my office. Never leave home without them!"

– Teo Ser Luck; Mayor, North East District; Senior Parliamentary Secretary, Ministry of Community Youth and Sports, and Ministry of Transport; Ironman triathlete and marathoner; devoted husband and father

"I continue my training even when overseas, whether for work or holiday. And even when I'm 3,200 m above sea level, amidst the rugged mountains of Bhutan." – Ben Tan

ALTITUDE TRAINING

Oxygen is transported from the lungs to the muscles by haemoglobin in the blood. Training at high altitude, where the air is rarified, induces a compensatory increase in the haemoglobin, thereby giving the runner a competitive advantage. While living at a high altitude will increase the haemoglobin levels, training at a high altitude limits the training intensity due to the lower amount of oxygen in the air. Therefore, in the early 1990's, American Drs Levine and Stray-Gundersen developed the "live high, train low" method whereby athletes live at altitude for about four weeks to increase their haemoglobin, while travelling down to a lower altitude for a few hours each day to train intensively. This allows the athlete to gain the best of both worlds.

This method was further modified by the American National Marathon Team in preparation for the 2004 Athens Olympic Games. The American runners lived and trained at moderate intensity at altitude, doing their base runs and travelled to low altitude for their high intensity workouts. They enjoyed unprecedented success by winning the men's silver and the women's bronze medals.

For convenience, the Finnish developed the 'Nitrogen Apartment,' whereby nitrogen is pumped into the room to displace oxygen, thus simulating the low-oxygen environment equivalent to an elevation of about 2,500 m. This allows their athletes to "live high, train low" without the need to travel abroad. The oxygen tent, which also artificially creates a low-oxygen environment, employs the same concept. However, these "artificial environments" work only if the athletes live in them for at least 20 to 22 hours a day at an equivalent altitude of 2,000 m to 2, 500 m for at least four consecutive weeks. This explains why oxygen tents, which do not make for comfortable living, do not work as well as the more spacious nitrogen apartment.

In another variation, runners living at sea level are intermittently exposed to low-oxygen air. This is termed Intermittent Hypoxic Exposure (IHE). Examples of devices that deliver low-oxygen air are the Go2Altitude Hypoxicator and the Altitrainer 200. However, the major flaw of IHE is the insufficient dose and duration of hypoxic conditions administered to be effective in inducing the production of haemoglobin.

05. RUN LIKE A KENYAN

For a long time, endurance runners and their exercise physiologists were fixated on improving maximal aerobic capacity ($\dot{V}O_{2}max$), as it is a known determinant of performance in distance running. The maximal aerobic capacity can be improved by up to 20 per cent. It was noted that after reaching a plateau in the maximal aerobic capacity, runners continued to improve their running times even though the maximal aerobic capacity remained unchanged. What were the changes occurring in the body that allowed running performance to continue to improve? Sports scientists now attribute the continued performance gains to improvements in lactate threshold and running economy.

RUNNING ECONOMY

Running requires energy. Running economy is defined as the energy demand for a given running speed, and is determined by measuring the consumption of oxygen. Taking body mass into consideration, runners with good running economy use less energy and therefore, less oxygen than runners with poor running economy at the same speed (i.e. for running economy, the lower the figure, the better the economy).

To illustrate the importance of running economy, let us compare my physiological profile with that of my running partner, Benny Goh. We have similar marathon personal best times:

Runner	Personal Best (hours)	$\dot{V}O_{2}max$ (ml/kg/min)	Speed at OBLA (km/h)	Running Economy at 13 km/h (ml/km/min)
B Tan	2:56	70.0	13.3	263
B Goh	2:52	64.2	15.5	208

Notice that although I have a higher relative $\dot{V}O_{2}max$, Benny has a higher onset of blood lactate accumulation (OBLA, or lactate threshold 2), i.e. he is able to run faster before triggering an unsustainable accumulation of lactic acid in the blood. Benny also has a better running economy, and most importantly, a faster personal best. With a higher running economy, a runner can more than compensate for a lower maximal aerobic capacity.

There are two main factors that can improve running economy: strength and running technique. Resistance training, speed intervals, and hill training can enhance strength in runners. Let us now look at how running technique can be improved.

RUNNING TECHNIQUE

We all know how to walk and run, or at least that is what we assume. The running gait is more complex than we think — it comprises complex and interlinked movements that require perfect coordination; the forces generated during running work in multiple planes; and some of the muscles involved control not one but two joints, making the neuromuscular control even more complex.

Is there only one 'correct' way to run? There is a correct running technique that we should aim for, as technique affects performance. But at the same time, there are inter-individual differences in the running gait that does not affect performance — these have to do with personal style rather than technique, and do not need to be corrected.

Running Gait Cycle

Before we discuss running techniques that will improve running economy, let us first look at the normal running gait cycle to familiarize with the commonly used terminology (figure 5.1).

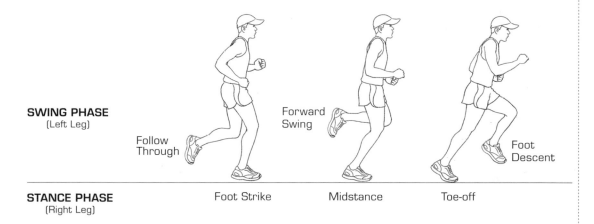

Figure 5.1. The swing and stance phase of the running gait cycle. Footstrike is the point at which the foot makes contact with the ground; toe off is the point when the foot leaves the ground; stance phase is in between those two points; mid stance is the point during the stance phase when the two knees are exactly side by side.

The limb that is in contact with the ground is in the stance phase, while the limb that is off the ground is in the swing phase. The stance phase comprises the foot strike, midstance, and toe-off. The swing phase comprises the follow through, forward swing, and foot descent. After the toe-off of the rear leg and before the foot strike of the forward leg, neither foot is in contact with the ground, and this is called the float phase. A step is the advancement of a single foot, and a stride comprises two steps.

The body movements during the gait cycle are described with reference to three planes, the saggital, coronal, and axial planes (figure 5.2)

Recycling of Energy

After foot strike, a ground reaction force (rebound) is generated. This rebound upon impact is crucial — if stored and subsequently released effectively, it helps propel the next step. In this way, the ground reaction forces generated from one step can be recycled, and this recycling provides half the energy required for running. This is why we save more energy taking a series of steps in succession compared to taking individual, isolated steps.

The sprinter recycles the energy from the rebound to increase the thrust of the next step, while the distance runner recycles the energy to conserve energy and therefore improve running economy.

To optimise recycling of energy, the runner needs to:

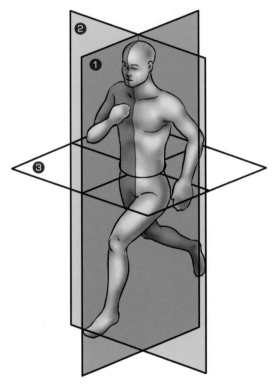

Figure 5.2. The (1) saggital, (2) coronal, and (3) axial planes of the body.

- Generate a good rebound. When running on sand, the rebound is dampened, and that is why it is much more tiring to run on sand.

- Store and release the energy from the rebound. The elasticity of the tendons and muscles act like springs to achieve this, through the stretch-shorten cycle. Likewise, the pendular oscillations of the limbs, vertical displacement of the body, and trunk torsion offer important means of storing and releasing energy.

The recycling of energy during running is the key concept that will help us understand how best to run in order to maximize running economy.

ACHILLES TENDON AND RUNNING

The Achilles tendon extends high up within the belly of the calf muscles, and is about 37 cm long. It is an elastic structure, lengthening by about 5 per cent during the midstance, when the tension can reach up to seven times the bodyweight.

During the recoil, the tendon returns about 35 per cent of the total energy that went into the loading phase, making it one of the more important structures for the recycling of energy during running.

The Economical Running Technique

There are certain aspects of running technique that affect running economy. These are discussed below.

CORRECT TECHNIQUE   **WRONG TECHNIQUE** ☒

KNEE SHOULD BE SLIGHTLY BENT (I.E. HIGHER KNEE LIFT) AT THE END OF THE FORWARD SWING

In the attempt to open the stride, some runners resort to extending the knee fully. This is disadvantageous, as it would result in the foot striking the ground in front of the body's centre of gravity. When the foot lands too far in front of the centre of mass, the ground reaction force acts as a brake to retard forward movement.

Driving the elbows further back would encourage a higher knee lift.

keep knee flexed at end of forward swing

Extending the knee at end of forward swing will tend to apply a braking force

LAND WITH FOOT UNDER CENTRE OF MASS

The foot should be under the centre of mass on impact with the ground, otherwise it acts as a brake.

(Foot strike under pelvis)　　(Foot strike too far in front of pelvis)

LEAN BODY SLIGHTLY FORWARD

At midstance, the ground reaction force is significant, so it should be directed in a forward rather than a purely upward direction. Leaning forward will also help reduce excessive vertical displacement.

The shoulder, hip, and ankle should be in a straight line during midstance. Do not bend over.

(Body leaning forward)　　(Body far too upright)

AVOID EXCESSIVE VERTICAL DISPLACEMENT

Some vertical displacement is necessary to recycle energy. Excessive vertical displacement is a waste of energy that could have been used for forward propulsion.

Vertical displacement can be minimized by leaning forward and by increasing the cadence.

Minimal vertical displacement

Excessive vertical displacement

BRING FOOT FROM TOE-OFF TO FOOT DESCENT IN AS DIRECT A PATH AS POSSIBLE

Avoid lifting the foot excessively towards the buttocks during the follow through, as this roundabout route during the forward swing wastes energy.

Minimal knee flexion during forward swing

Excessive butt-kick

OPTIMISE TRUNK TORSION TO RECYCLE ENERGY

While activating the core muscles, rotate the pelvis and shoulders (in the axial plane) in the opposite directions. This twisting action is an important mechanism for recycling energy. It also helps to open the stride without the need to land with the foot in front of the centre of mass.

If the shoulder and hip on the same side move in the same direction, this is called trunk rotation. Such a movement is unwieldy and wastes energy

Maximal trunk torsion _Minimal trunk torsion_

KEEP LOWER LIMBS IN THE SAGITTAL PLANE DURING FORWARD SWING

Movements of the lower or upper limbs too far away from the sagittal plane is a waste of energy, as such movements do not contribute much to forward propulsion.

Limb in saggital plane during forward swing _Foot swinging out during forward swing_

Foot Strike

Which is the optimal foot strike — heel, midfoot, or forefoot? Recall that the emphasis is on generating a good rebound. Whichever type of foot strike that generates the best rebound for that particular runner would be the right one. Each runner will need to feel the rebound and select whichever gives him the best rebound. A good rebound is not necessarily the one with the loudest footstep — it is the one that gives a firm, crisp 'thump,' rather than a slapping or sliding sound.

Generally, a heel strike tends to be associated with a foot that is landing too far forward; a forefoot strike tends to stress the calves and Achilles tendon (especially for runners who are unaccustomed to landing on the forefoot); a midfoot strike tends to be spared of the faults of the other two and gives a good rebound. Having said that, these are only generalisations — each runner has to feel what is right for him or her.

Stride and Cadence

Elite marathoners can cruise at an average speed of 20 km/h. Most of us cannot even sprint at that speed. How do the elite runners manage to go so fast and appear to be cruising rather than sprinting? They do not appear to be sprinting because they have a low cadence, (compared to that of a sprinter), short ground contact time (i.e. short stance phase), long stride length, and long float phase. A stride comprises two steps: from the time one foot makes contact with the ground, to the next time the same foot hits the ground again. Cadence on the other hand, refers to the number of steps a runner takes per minute. During the float phase, elite runners 'fly' further than weaker runners because they have a very strong rebound.

What is the optimal cadence for distance running? Recall how the resonant frequency of the pendulum is dependent on its length? The longer the pendulum, the lower the resonant frequency. Swinging the pendulum at its resonant frequency requires minimal effort. Swinging the pendulum faster or lower than the resonant frequency requires more effort. Likewise, the running movement has a certain 'resonant frequency' or cadence which feels natural and effortless. Taller individuals are more suited to a lower cadence while shorter runners are more comfortable with a higher cadence. Each runner will need to feel what cadence suits him or her best — there is no one-size-fits-all cadence.

Video Gait Analysis

It is difficult for a runner to analyse his own gait. Getting a friend to video your running gait, either running on a treadmill or outdoors, would be helpful. The best way would be to undergo a video gait analysis, where frame-by-frame analysis using computer software allows joint angles and displacements to be measured. Accompanying a video gait analysis, you will need an experienced sports physician, biomechanist, physiologist, podiatrist, or trainer that is familiar with gait analysis so that you can identify faults and take corrective action.

Changing Gears

There is no single technique that is optimal for uphill running, downhill running, cruising, and sprinting to the finish. The optimal technique changes slightly, depending on the gradient and running speed.

It is useful to practice different running 'modes,' so that you can effectively switch gears to suit various stretches of the course:

- **Uphill Running.** Shorten the stride and increase the cadence. Lift the knees higher while driving the elbows further back. Lean further forward.

- **Downhill Running.** Open up the stride by rotating the pelvis more. You can extend the knees further, but short of full extension. Passively 'roll' down the hill to conserve energy — resist extending the knees fully and applying the brakes.

- **Stepping Up the Pace.** During the race, you may need to pick up speed over short stretches, e.g. to overtake or 'sprint' to the finish. Lift the knees higher, drive the elbows further back, lean slightly further forward, reduce pelvic rotation, and increase the cadence.

When running uphill or stepping up the pace, be careful not to go full throttle as it will lead to a build up of lactate, and that will take a long time to clear.

Training to Improve Running Technique

Just as it is not easy to break a habit, it is also difficult to correct a faulty running technique. Regular practice and constant reminders are necessary. Running drills, pace runs, tempo runs, aerobic intervals, speed intervals, and hill training can all be used to improve running technique. To practice 'switching gears,' cross-country running is ideal. Indeed, many of the top African marathoners started their athletic careers as cross-country runners.

Watch how top marathoners run and take a mental picture of it. Visualize it in your mind regularly to reinforce the ideal technique. Visualize it even while running, especially when you are fatigued, to resume the desired running form. I recall watching the 2004 Olympic

Marathon race on television late one night, and I was impressed with the running form of the leader of the pack. I memorized it and visualised it during my 12 km training run the next morning. It was only a base run, and I did not push myself at all. Furthermore, I had very little sleep that night as the race telecast was in the wee hours of the morning. When I checked my watch at the end of run, I was surprised that I had cut six minutes off my personal best for that 12 km course!

To adopt a good running technique or form, the runner needs to be guided by feel. Feel the rebound and the cadence — you will know when you hit the 'sweet spot.'

Running Technique and Injuries

Unfortunately the fastest running technique is not synonymous with the safest running technique — there is a trade-off between speed and safety. The faster techniques generate higher impact forces and are more likely to lead to injuries. Hence, progressive training is necessary to allow the body time to adapt to these higher forces. Running injuries are discussed in further detail in Chapter 9.

"I've run 12 marathons and an ultra-marathon. The one thing I've learned to focus on when fatigue sets in during the last few kilometres of the race is my posture and running form. Keeping a good running form has helped me to cross the finish line faster than if I drag my feet to the end."

Tan Swee Kheng, Kinesiologist & movement specialist, avid runner with a marathon personal best of 3:29

♥ 06. NUTRITION FOR DISTANCE RUNNERS
>>With input from Ling Ping Sing & Fabian Lim

A proper nutrition plan is essential to maximize your training adaptations and competition performance. With an increase in training volume, the body's nutrient requirements also increase. There are several pertinent nutritional considerations that relate to running performance:

- Depletion of muscle glycogen stores and consequent low blood sugar (hypoglycaemia), will cause central nervous system fatigue and deprive exercising muscle of fuel especially during a distance race

- Dehydration

- Gastrointestinal discomfort. During endurance races, the digestive system has to compete with the working muscles for blood, and with priority going to the muscles, the digestive tract often does not function optimally, making it difficult to ingest and absorb the food and fluids we take

- Mineral deficiency e.g. iron or calcium

- Electrolyte imbalance e.g. sodium

MACRO- AND MICRONUTRIENTS
In order to use nutrition as a tool to improve your performance, you must first understand your body's nutritional needs during exercise. Let us look at the requirements in terms of macronutrients (carbohydrates, proteins, fat), micronutrients (vitamins, minerals, antioxidants), and fluids.

Carbohydrates
Carbohydrates comprise glucose and glycogen. Glycogen is made up of many molecules of glucose, and serves as a storage depot for glucose. Our bodies can use carbohydrate, fat, and protein, in that order of preference, as fuel sources — hence, these macronutrients are also called energy substrates. At rest, we tend to use fat as the main energy source. Fat is mobilised slowly, but this slow rate is fine as the body consumes calories slowly while at rest. Take my body's energy substrate utilisation for example (I weigh 64 kg) — when I am resting, an analysis of my respiratory gases (i.e. oxygen and carbon dioxide) shows that I have a resting metabolic rate of 1,427 kcal/day (i.e. my body expends 1,427 kcal per day if I sleep all day), and that 56 per cent of this energy comes from burning fat and 44 per cent from carbohydrates (see figure 6.1). When we start exercising, our muscles burn calories at a faster rate. Because there is a limit to how fast body fat can be released,

the body becomes more dependent on carbohydrate as a fuel substrate, especially at exercise intensities exceeding 70 per cent of $\dot{V}O_{2max}$. The figure below (figure 6.2) demonstrates the increasing use of glucose by the muscles as the intensity and duration of exercise increases. When I run at 14 km/h during a marathon, respiratory gas analysis shows that I expend 1,155 kcal per hour, with 68 per cent of my energy needs supplied by carbohydrates and 32 per cent by fat.

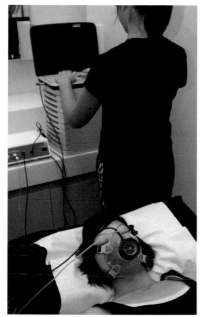

Figure 6.1. A subject undergoing a resting metabolic rate measurement at the Singapore Sports Medicine Centre

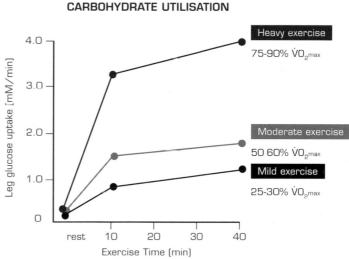

Figure 6.2. Carbohydrate utilisation at various exercise intensities and duration.

Carbohydrates can be mobilised quickly to meet the muscles' needs, but unfortunately, its stores are limited. A 70-kg individual running at 10 km/h will require slightly more than 3,000 kcal of energy to complete a marathon. However, the average person has 600 g of carbohydrate stores in the muscle and liver (see figure 6.3), providing only 2,400 kcal of energy (1 g of carbohydrates produces 4 kcal of energy). Another estimate places the glycogen stores at 1,800 kcal and 1,550 kcal for well-trained male (averaging 68 kg) and female (averaging 54 kg) endurance runners. From these estimates, we can see that the carbohydrate store is insufficient for the whole marathon.

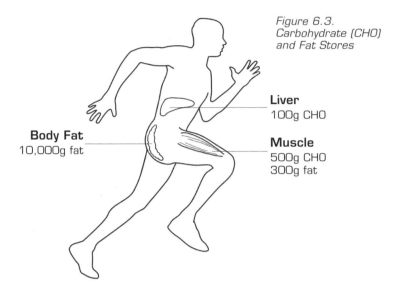

Figure 6.3.
Carbohydrate (CHO)
and Fat Stores

Liver
100g CHO

Body Fat
10,000g fat

Muscle
500g CHO
300g fat

When our carbohydrate stores are depleted at around the 30 km mark or 3 hrs 20 mins into the race, we 'hit the wall.' To overcome this, marathon runners will need to:

- Boost their carbohydrate stores through regular training and pre-race carbohydrate loading

- Replenish carbohydrates during the race, and

- Train the body to be better at mobilising the fat stores during the run, thereby sparing the carbohydrates such that they last longer

Regular training and increasing your mileage helps to enhance the carbohydrate stores by about 10 per cent. The increase is especially marked in untrained runners, since they are starting from a low baseline. But to tolerate the high training mileages, we need to have enough carbohydrates during training. Your daily carbohydrate requirement is based on your training load i.e. intensity, duration, and frequency:

- Moderate to low intensity exercise: 5 – 7g Carbohydrate per kg body weight (BW)

- Moderate to high indensity exercise: 7 – 10g Carbohydrate per kg BW

- Extreme exercise that last more than four hours per session: 10 – 12g Carbohydrate per kg BW

- 0 – 4 hours immediately after exercise: 1g per kg BW per hour, at frequent intervals

It is important to have sufficient carbohydrate before, during and after training to maximize the performance. We will discuss how to replenish your carbohydrate stores during a race, later in this chapter. After racing and training, replenishing your carbohydrate stores quickly, by ingesting carbohydrates within 30 minutes after training, enhances recovery and reduces fatigue.

Protein

During training, microtrauma occurs in our musculoskeletal system, but as part of the adaptation process, we repair the microtrauma at the same time. If our training stimulus is optimal, the rate of repair 'overshoots' the rate of microtrauma, and we get stronger, fitter, and even more resilient to injuries. But if the rate of repair lags behind, then we suffer overuse injuries. Protein intake is critical in ensuring adequate repair and recovery, as much of our muscles, tendons, and bones are made up of proteins.

Protein is also a minor fuel source for the muscles. If our carbohydrate intake is adequate, then we spare the protein and can better channel it towards repair and recovery. Hence, those who are on extreme diets tend to lose lean body mass, and this is certainly counterproductive to peak performance.

The recommended daily allowance for the general population is 0.8 g of protein per kilogramme body weight. For the endurance athlete, the research consensus is to increase the protein intake to 1.2 g to 1.6 g of protein per kilogramme of body weight. With a healthy, balanced diet you should be able to meet the increased protein requirement without the need for protein supplements. Bodybuilders, on the other hand, have a higher requirement of 1.8 g of protein per kilogramme body weight, and protein supplements are usually required to achieve such levels.

Some studies have found that the combination of carbohydrate and protein intake after exercise enhances the protein uptake compared to ingesting protein alone. Therefore, a balance diet is recommended.

The dangers of an excessively high protein intake include:

- Not getting enough carbohydrate to meet energy needs. This may cause the body to use protein as an energy source, resulting in muscle wasting.
- Urinary frequency places an undue load on the kidneys and also risks dehydration
- May increase urinary calcium loss
- Increased fat consumption, because most high protein foods tend to be high in fat as well

Fat

At rest, our body relies mostly on fat as an energy source. As exercise intensity increases, carbohydrates contribute an increasingly higher proportion of the energy relative to fat. While the proportion of fat utilisation diminishes, the absolute amount of fat oxidation actually increases with increasing exercise intensity, due to the higher overall energy expenditure. Well-trained endurance athletes are better at mobilizing fat than untrained individuals, and hence they are able to tap on a larger total pool of energy reserves and exercise for longer durations.

Although fat is a significant energy source, endurance runners do not have to make a conscious effort to accumulate fat stores. The reasons are, firstly, that there is a substantial amount fat in our diet. Someone who does not pay special attention to his/her diet may have about 40 per cent of their calories coming from fat. If you consciously avoid excessive fat intake, your fat intake may be reduced to the recommended under-30 per cent. If you can reduce this to 20 per cent, you would have done exceptionally well. The second reason is that our pre-existing fat stores are sufficient for our training and competition needs, even if we are quite lean. Take for example a lean, 65 kg endurance runner with 15 per cent body fat. He would have 9.8 kg of body fat, and since each kilogramme of body fat can deliver 7,700 kcal, he would have a fat store that is worth over 75,000 kcal! He only needs about 3,000 kcal to run a marathon (if all the energy for running the marathon were to come from fat, and this is clearly not the case), or about 3,000 kcal per day to sustain his bodily functions and training needs.

Fat is stored not only under the skin (subcutaneous fat) where it is visible, but it is also stored around your internal organs (intraabdominal or visceral fat) and within your muscle cells (intramuscular fat). Intraabdominal fat is strongly associated with chronic diseases like diabetes and hypertension, and exercise is an effective way to remove excessive intrabdominal fat. Both subcutaneous and intraabdominal fat represent 'dead weight' that the runner has to carry around while running, slowing him down. Intramuscular fat, on the other hand, is more useful to the runner, as it can be mobilized faster and help supplement carbohydrates as an energy source during exercise.

Micronutrients: Vitamins, Minerals and Anti-oxidants

Micronutrients are required by the body in small amounts for optimal function. Iron, for example, is a micronutrient that is required for the production of haemoglobin and oxidative enzymes, and is thus important for endurance athletes. Adequate intake of vitamin and minerals is important for optimal health and maintain performance.

Dietary surveys show that most runners are able to meet their daily vitamin and mineral requirements without supplementation. With a balanced, wholesome diet encompassing the recommended two servings of fruits and vegetables daily, it is unlikely that you will suffer any nutritional deficiencies. But if you want to play it even safer, you can supplement your diet with a multivitamin daily.

Do bear in mind that the body requires nutrients in an optimal range — too little and you suffer nutritional deficiencies; too much and you suffer toxicities and place an extra load on your body to try to remove the excess. Excessive vitamin A, for example, is toxic. By taking lots of vitamins and minerals, all you are doing is producing expensive urine. You benefit from supplementation only if you are lacking in certain vitamins or minerals.

There is no evidence that increasing training loads will increase the requirement for anti-oxidants. Therefore, it is not necessary to supplement your diet with anti-oxidants if you are eating a wide variety of food.

Fluids

Water is important for sustaining a high cardiac output and for preventing the body from overheating during exercise. While running, we lose water through our expired air, skin (perspiration), and our kidneys. If fluid intake is not able to match fluid loss, we become increasingly dehydrated. Our body will attempt to conserve water by producing less urine, but we will continue to sweat, as the body needs to prevent itself from overheating. With greater degrees of dehydration, our cardiac output starts to drop, our performance deteriorates, and we eventually stop sweating and begin to overheat.

The simplest way to assess the degree of dehydration is to track changes in bodyweight. Each kilogramme of weight loss during exercise is equivalent to 1 L of fluid deficit. Runners can tolerate up to 2 per cent of dehydration (i.e. 1.2 kg of water losses for a 60 kg runner) without much consequences. When fluid losses exceed 2 per cent of bodyweight, performance can be impaired by up to 20 per cent. Hence, it pays to be well hydrated before, during and after running. Depending on the degree of dehydration, you may need four to 24 hours to completely replace your fluid losses.

While dehydration compromises performance and puts you at risk of heat injuries, over-hydration is dangerous and can be fatal. Excessive fluid intake dilutes the blood, thereby reducing the plasma concentration of sodium and resulting in hyponatremia. Hyponatraemia causes the brain to swell, resulting in coma and eventually death. Slower runners are more prone to dilutional hyponatraemia as the slow pace allows the runner to drink amply.

To avoid under- or over-hydrating, our fluid replacement needs to match our fluid losses. You can calculate your total fluid losses by following the steps below:

1. Weigh yourself before and after at least one hour of running under conditions similar to competition or a hard training session

2. Weigh barefooted, with minimal clothing. For the post-exercise weighing, be sure to towel dry and weigh as soon as is practical after running (e.g. less than 10 min)

3. Total fluid loss (in litres) = bodyweight before exercise (in kg) – bodyweight after exercise + fluid consumed during the exercise (in litres)

For example, if you weigh 60 kg before running and 59 kg after running for an hour, and you drank 0.5 L of water during the run, then your total fluid loss is 1.5 L per hour. Your degree of dehydration would be (60-59) x 100 / 60 = 1.7 per cent

To limit dehydration during a distance race, follow these tips:

- It is a good habit to drink regularly throughout the day

- Two to four hours before the race, drink 400 – 700 ml of fluid

- Drink 150 – 250 ml of fluid at regular intervals during the race to match your fluid loss. Alternatively, work out how much you need to drink at each water station in order to match your fluid loss. You will notice that it is quite difficult to match your intake to your fluid loss during a marathon — if unable to do so, then do the best you can and ensure that at the end of the race, you are not more than 2 per cent dehydrated. It takes some practice to be able to tolerate drinking the intended amount of fluid at each drink station.

- After the race, weigh yourself to determine how dehydrated you are, and replace 150 per cent of your fluid deficit over two to six hours, e.g. for 1 kg of fluid lost, replace with 1.5 L of fluid

- Do not depend on your thirst — if you drink just enough to satisfy your thirst, you are replacing only approximately $2/3$ of your fluid losses

- Check your urine colour — it should be almost colourless two hours after the run

During exercise, blood is shunted away from the gut to the exercising muscles. The gut is even more deprived of blood when we are dehydrated, and this disturbs intestinal motility and slows gastric emptying rate. A high gastric emptying rate ensures that ingested fluid passes through the stomach quickly and into the small intestines where absorption can occur. Otherwise, the fluid sits in your stomach, sloshing around and causing abdominal discomfort. As dehydration slows down gastric emptying and fluid absorption, it is best to hydrate well before we become dehydrated.

What is the best fluid to drink during and after running? Generally, for low intensity running of less than 90 minutes, plain water will suffice. However, with higher intensities and durations exceeding 90 minutes, sports drinks are generally recommended.

Sport drinks contain 5 – 8 per cent of sugars and some electrolytes (e.g. sodium and potassium in specific concentrations). The sugars help provide some energy (not very much), while the electrolytes help replace that lost through our sweat. The sugars and salts in the right concentrations optimise gastric emptying rate. Chilling the sports drink further enhances gastric emptying. But which brand of sports drink should we use? If you look at the nutritional labelling of the sports drink, you will notice that the sugar and salt concentrations are all very similar. The major difference between brands is the flavouring. Hence, the brand you use is not particularly critical. By choosing a brand that is most palatable to you, you will be encouraged to drink more and minimize the risk of dehydration. Before a major race, do find out which brand of sports drink will be provided at the drink stations, and use that brand during practice to get yourself accustomed to it.

Soft drinks, fruit juices, and cordials are not the best replacement fluids as the high sugar concentration delays gastric emptying. Some energy drinks are not good replacement fluids during exercise due to their high osmolarity, or concentration, (as much as five times greater than sport drinks). Avoid alcohol for 24 hours after exercise — alcohol acts as a diuretic and interferes with rehydration and other recovery processes.

NUTRITION FOR TRAINING AND RACING

Now let us take a look at nutritional strategies during the training phase, as well as just before, during and after a race.

Nutrition Strategies for Training

The distance runner's training involves a fair amount of mileage, and this increases his nutritional needs. Therefore, a balanced diet that is high in carbohydrate and moderate in protein, with plenty of fruits and vegetables can supply the runner with sufficient energy, vitamins and minerals, as well as material for repair and adaptation. Prompt refuelling and rehydration after a training session promotes rapid recovery, enabling the runner to put in even more quality training at the next training session.

Follow the carbohydrate target in the table below (a sample training meal plan for a 60-kg male aiming for 420 – 600g of carbohydrates (CHO) per day) to ensure sufficient fuel for your body. Include a carbohydrate rich snack before and after each training session to help restore the muscle and liver glycogen stores. Try to consume sport drinks that can provide 30 – 60g of carbohydrate each hour to maintain adequate blood glucose.

Meals	Suggested Menu	CHO (g)
Breakfast	White bread x 4 slices with jam x 1 tablespoon Banana x 1 medium Low fat milk x 300 ml	105
Snack (Before Exercise)	Cereal bar x 1 Soy milk x 200 ml	35
During Endurance Exercise for 2 hour	Sport drink x 200 ml every ½ hour Power gel x 1 sachet	75
Snack (Post exercise 1st hour)	Tuna bun x 1 Fruit juice x 250 ml Watermelon x 1 slice	60
Snack (Post exercise 2nd hour)	Raisin bread x 1 slice Milk shake x 300 ml (250 ml low fat milk with 1 fruit and tablespoon honey)	60
Lunch	Rice x 1.5 cups Meat/poultry/fish x 200 g (Lean meat without skin) Vegetables x 1 small bowl Orange x 1 medium Fruit juice x 250 ml	105
Dinner	Fish slice noodle soup Papaya x 2 slices	70
Supper	Fruit yoghurt x 200 g	30
	Total:	540

The table above is just an example — you can work with your sports nutritionist to devise a training menu that is tailored to your individual training needs, food preferences and training schedule. Use the training phase to try out the food and fluids you intend to use before and during the race.

Nutrition Strategies for Competition

Carbohydrate Loading. For endurance events, it pays to start the race with your fuel tank fully loaded. Runners do this via carbohydrate loading. Carbohydrate loading takes various forms — the early version is a six-day regimen just before a race, comprising three days of 'starvation' to induce the storage enzymes, followed by three days of increased carbohydrate intake. As the first three days stresses the runner at a time when he needs to recharge in time for the race, it may compromise performance. Hence, most runners skip the first phase and simply increase their carbohydrate intake in the three days leading up to the race.

Exercise durations lasting more than 90 minutes will benefit from carbohydrate loading. When done effectively, carbohydrate loading can increase the runner's muscle glycogen stores by 50 – 100 per cent thereby delaying fatigue and helping to sustain a high exercise intensity over a longer duration.

To carbo-load, the carbohydrate intake should be increased to 8 – 12g of carbohydrate per kilogramme of bodyweight per day. For example, a 60-kg runner should aim for a carbohydrate intake of 480 – 720g of carbohydrate per day. Minimize fat intake and replace fat with carbohydrate, e.g. using jam as spread rather than margarine. Supplement with meal replacements during this period if you have difficulty increasing your intake.

Hydration is important during the carbo-loading phase, as glycogen storage has been shown to be more effective when accompanied by an increased water intake. Drink sufficient water to suppress the thirst sensation and to maintain a clear urine colour throughout the day. Urine colour can be affected by medication and dietary supplement (e.g., vitamin C, B) intake.

During the three-day carbo-loading phase, the training volume should be tapered down to approximately 20 minutes per day for two days and then resting completely on the day before the race.

The day before the race, avoid excessively fatty as well as high-residue foods (e.g. vegetables) as they tend to sit in the digestive system longer, adding to your bodyweight and increasing the risk of abdominal discomfort during the race. Take familiar carbohydrate products and stick to water during the evening meal, avoiding caffeine-containing beverages that may lead to insomnia. If you do not have high blood pressure, salt your food generously.

The following is a sample meal plan for a 60-kg runner during the carbo-loading phase, aiming for 480 – 720g of CHO per day:

Meals	Suggested Menu	CHO (g)
Breakfast	Frosted cornflakes x 2 cups Low fat milk x 250 ml Bread x 2 slices with 2 tablespoons of jam Banana x 1 medium-sized	150
Snack	Biscuit x 2 pieces Fruit juice x 500 ml	50
Lunch	Rice x 2 cup Fruit yoghurt x 200 g Squash or fruit flavoured drink x 200 ml	150
Snack	Pancake x 2 medium Maple syrup x 1 tablespoon	50
Dinner	Pasta x 2 cups Fruit salad x 2 cups Ice cream x 2 cups Sport drink x 500 ml	200
Snack	Fruit smoothies x 250 ml (250 ml low fat milk + 1 fruit + 1 tablespoon of honey)	50
	Total:	650

Pre-Competition Meals and Drinks. Have a light carbohydrate snack containing 1 – 4 g of carbohydrate per kilogramme of bodyweight, at least one to six hours prior to the race. During the training phase, do try out how close to the run you can afford to eat, as this varies from individual to individual. The last meal/snack before the race should be high in carbohydrates and low in fat and fibre. If you are prone to nervous diarrhoea, a light meal such as liquid meal replacement, sports bar or drink, and milkshake may be easier to tolerate. Always remember to test out your pre-competition meal during your training, and choose the food, amount, and time interval that you can tolerate comfortably. Do not try something new before the race.

Here are some pre-competition meal ideas:

- **2 hours or less before competition**
  - Sport drink/fruit juice
  - Liquid meal replacement
  - Low fat yogurt
  - Fresh fruit
  - Cereal bar
  - White bread with jam/honey

- **2 – 4 hours before competition**
  - Low fibre cereal with low fat milk
  - Waffles/pancakes with jam/syrup
  - *Chee cheong fun* with sweet sauce (no oil)
  - Tomato-based pasta
  - Noodle soup with less vegetables
  - Baked potatoes
  - Sandwiches or bun with low fat fillings

Start the race well-hydrated — drink 400 – 700 millilitres (ml) of fluid two to four hours before the competition. This will allow enough time for urination of excess fluid. Aim to take another 300 – 600 ml of fluid within 15 minutes before the start.

Eating and Drinking on the Run. Our body's carbohydrate, water, salts may not remain at optimal levels through to the end of the marathon or even the half-marathon. Hence, you may need to replenish them during the race. Sport drinks, gels and bars are formulated to be tolerable during exercise. Find out the specific sports drink or energy supplement that will be provided by the event organiser during the race, so that you can try them out during training and have time to get accustomed to them.

Aim to consume 30 – 60 g of carbohydrates per hour and drink at a comfortable amount of 150 – 250 ml fluid each time. Each of the competition drink/snack serving below provides about 30 g of carbohydrate:

- 500 ml sport drink
- 300 ml cola drink
- 1 packet sport sachet
- 1.5 cereal bars
- 1 large banana

To work out your hydration strategy, you will need to know your sweat rate and the number of water points there will be during the race. For example, a 60 kg, 4-hour marathon runner with a sweat rate of 1 L per hour will lose 4 L of water during a marathon. He can afford to be 2 per cent dehydrated at most, meaning that his water deficit should not exceed 1.2 L at the finish. Hence, he will need to consume 4 – 1.2 = 2.8 litres of fluids during the race. If there are drink stations every 3 km, then there will be about 13 drink stations, so the runner will need to consume at least 215 ml of fluids at each drink station. Sometimes, the race organizers will inform you of the size of the paper cups that will be provided, so you can work out how many cups you will need to drink at each station.

Drinking on the run is not easy, as spillage is common. To minimise spillage:

1. Slow down a little as you reach the drink station

2. Grab the cup firmly and steady it rather than drink immediately, as you keep running

3. Use your index finger and thumb to close the mouth of the cup, leaving only small opening to drink from

Working out how much energy you need while on the run is less straightforward, as it depends on your rate of energy expenditure, your substrate utilisation (proportion of carbohydrate and fat contribution to your energy needs), and the size of your carbohydrate stores. While the first two can be determined through exercise testing, the third is difficult to determine. Suffice to say that if you do 'hit the wall' during a marathon race, you will benefit from consuming carbohydrates during the run. If you have a choice, consume sports drinks rather than water during the race — not only does it provide you with a little calories, it is also easier to assimilate. Using the above example, if you consume 2.8 L of sports drinks containing 6 per cent sugar during the race, that would provide you with 2,800 ml x 6 per cent = 168 g of carbohydrates or 672 kcal or energy. If sports drinks were available only at alternate drink stations, then you would be getting 336 kcal during the race. You can supplement this with sports gels, which contain about 100 kcal per sachet. These gels are best consumed with water rather than sports drinks. There is a limit to the number of gel packs that you can comfortably tolerate (perhaps up to three) for a full marathon, so try them out during training to see what is a good number for you. Avoid waiting till you hit the wall before taking your first gel pack for the race.

Post-Competition Nutrition.   Aim to quickly replenish your fluid, carbohydrates, and electrolytes soon after the run. Proteins also help with recovery and repair. A carbohydrate-rich snack with some protein serves as an ideal for recovery snack. Consume 1 g of carbohydrate per kilogramme of bodyweight within 30 minutes after the race, followed by a high-carbohydrate meal in the next two to four hours. If a main meal is not available, have carbohydrate snacks (at least 50 g carbohydrates every two hours) until the next main meal. A small amount of protein, about 10 – 20 g, in the recovery meals can help increase the rate of muscle glycogen storage.

Examples of recovery snacks include:

- **Carbohydrate-focused:**
  - Sport drinks, fruit juice or soft drink
  - Banana sandwich
  - Fresh/canned fruit
  - Sweet muffin
  - Cereal bar

- **Carbohydrate + protein focused:**
  - Fruit smoothie
  - Cereal with milk and fruit
  - Sandwiches including meat/cheese/chicken filling
  - Meat/red bean bun

Immediately after the race, replace 150 per cent of your fluid deficit over two to six hours. Sport drinks are good recovery drinks as they help to replace water, carbohydrates, and electrolytes. You can replace your salt losses through the recovery snack and meal as well.

Avoid consuming excessive amounts of alcohol during the recovery period, as alcohol is a diuretic and interferes with re-hydration and other recovery processes. If you have to consume alcohol, delay the intake as long as you can and limit yourself to three standard drinks for men and two standard drinks for women.

SUPPLEMENTS AND SPORTS FOODS

There are many supplements in the market that claim to improve running performance, prevent fatigue, and increase energy supply. However, most of these supplements are not supported by sound research so you need to avoid being taken in by marketing ploys.

Supplements are beneficial if you are deficient or at risk of being deficient in that nutrient. For example, you may be too busy to have proper meals and are unable to meet the recommended daily intake of various vitamins or minerals. However, supplements should not replace wholesome food in the long run. If you are not deficient in the nutrient, supplementation may lead to toxicity.

Take protein supplements for example. Egg white is an excellent source of protein, as it contains all the essential amino acids and has a high bioavailability (i.e. easy to digest, absorb, and assimilate). However, you may not have time to prepare hard or half boiled eggs in the mornings and it is certainly challenging to get access to egg white immediately after training. This is where protein supplements, in the form of tablets or powders that can be mixed with water, provide a convenient alternative, albeit at a cost.

The table that follows shows some of the more legitimate sports food and supplements that may work for you:

Types of sports food/ supplement	Form	Composition	Function
Sports drink	Powder or liquid	• 5 – 8 per cent CHO • 10 – 25 mmol/L sodium • 3 – 5 mmol/L potassium	• Provide fluid and CHO during and after exercise. • Useful for rehydration and replacement of the electrolyte losses during exercise.
Sports gel	Gel	• 60 – 70 per cent CHO (~25g CHO per sachet). • Some contain MCTs or caffeine	• Provide source of CHO that is more convenient during exercise

Types of sports food/ supplement	Form	Composition	Function
Sport bar	Bar	• Consist of 40 – 50 g CHO with 5 – 10 g protein. • Usually low in fat and fibre. • Contains 50-100 per cent RDA of vitamin/mineral	• Convenient solid meal replacement for travel, before/after exercise. Consist of carbohydrate, protein, vitamin and mineral.
Liquid meal replacement	Powder or liquid	• 1 – 1.5 kcal/ml • 15 – 20 per cent protein • 50 – 70 per cent CHO • Low to moderate fat • 500 – 1000 ml can meet RDAs	• Supplement high energy/CHO/ nutrient diet. Meal replacement before exercise if prone to nervous diarrhoea.
Iron Supplement	Capsule/ tablet	• Ferrous sulfate/gluconate/ fumarate	• Supervised management of iron deficiency
Calcium supplement	Capsule/ tablet	• Calcium carbonate/ phosphate/lactate	• Calcium supplementation in low-energy or low dairy food diet. • Treatment/prevention of osteopenia
Vitamin/ mineral supplement	Capsule/ tablet	• Broad range • 1 – 4 times of RDAs	• Micronutrient support for restricted variety diets e.g. vegetarian diet, unreliable food supply e.g. traveling athlete, heavy competition schedule where normal eating patterns may be disrupted
Creatine	Powder	• Creatine monohydrate/ Phosphate/Citrate/Esters • Recommended dosage: 10 – 20 g per day for four to five days to load, and 2 – 3 g per day for maintenance	• Improve performance in single or multiple sprints, and may be helpful for your interval training sessions. • May gain muscle mass. • Normally found in meat and fish but the doses used are more than that found in normal foods.
Caffeine	Powder/ liquid/gels	• Coffee, cola drinks and some sports products • Recommended dosage: 1– 3 mg/kg	• Increase performance in prolonged exercise and may also be helpful in exercise of shorter duration. • Large dose may cause over-arousal and poor sleep pattern.
Bicarbonate	Powder	• Sodium bicarbonate • Recommended dosage: 0.3 g per kg body weight before exercise	• Can help to enhance performance for high intensity exercise lasting for one to eight minutes. • Risk of gastrointestinal upset.

CAN VEGETARIANS BE FAST RUNNERS?

The answer is, "Yes!" Animal sources of protein contain all the essential amino acids and are easier to digest and absorb compared to plant sources. However, vegetarian runners can get all the proteins and amino acids they need for recovery and adaptation if they consume a wide variety of protein-rich plant food. Nuts, seeds, legumes, soy product, and whole grains are good sources of plant protein. Recovery snacks that are rich in both proteins and carbohydrates include red bean buns, low-fat muesli bars, soymilk, peanut butter sandwiches and soy burgers.

Singapore's national record holder in the marathon, M. Rameshon, is a vegetarian. "Before I turned vegetarian at the age of 19 years, my personal best marathon time was 3:20 hours," says Rameshon. "At age 22, I cut my time down to 2:40 hours in my very first marathon after turning vegetarian! By eating smart and consuming a wide variety of fruits, vegetables, and grains, I felt strong and continued to improve, eventually achieving a personal best and the national record of 2:24 hours." Tay Wai Boon, a 38 year-old marathoner with a personal best of 3:04 hours (Singapore Marathon 2005) agrees, "I can comfortably handle a weekly mileage of 100 km per week while on a vegetarian diet. Carbo-loading is also easy for vegetarians."

07. WEIGHT MANAGEMENT FOR OPTIMAL PERFORMANCE

Running a marathon requires lots of energy, and since there is a plentiful supply of energy stored within our body fat, is it possible that being fat is advantageous to the marathon runner? A 60-kg female runner with a lean 15 per cent body fat has about 9 kg of fat or 69,300 kcal of energy stored up. That is much more than the 3,000 plus kcal she will need to complete her marathon! While there is a lot of energy stored up in our body fat, the challenge is in mobilising that fat quickly enough to meet the needs of our muscles while running. Although one can train the body to be better at mobilising fat during exercise, fat combustion uses more oxygen per calorie extracted, compared to carbohydrate. Carrying the extra weight from body fat lowers running economy, since additional calories are required to carry the excess weight. Body fat also impedes the dissipation of heat produced by our working muscles, increasing the runner's risk of heat injuries.

In addition to being difficult to mobilise, having a high oxygen cost per calorie expended, impairing running economy, and impeding heat dissipation, body fat, if excessive, can contribute to impact injuries. Hence, it is therefore not surprising that distance runners have among the lowest percentage of body fat mass compared to other sports — the average elite marathon runner has a percentage body fat of less than 10 per cent for male and less than 15 per cent for females.

To lose weight, one needs to incur an energy deficit, i.e. the energy expenditure must exceed the energy intake. The bigger the deficit, the faster the weight loss. However, if the deficit were excessive, then the runner would be too lethargic to put in any quality training, impair his recovery rate, lose lean body mass, and be prone to the consequences of immuosuppression (a less active immunune system) such as frequent upper respiratory tract infections. Hence, the runner who needs to lose weight will have to perform a balancing act between having an adequate energy deficit to lose weight, but have adequate energy to meet his training and recovery needs.

In shedding fat, lean body mass (muscle and bone mass) may be lost together with it as well. Fortunately for runners, this is minimised as the active use of the musculoskeletal system during running helps to preserve muscle and bone mass during weight loss, provided the calorie restriction is not too severe.

While a lean frame makes for a fast distance runner, weight loss should not be overdone. Being underweight (i.e. body mass index < 18.5 kg/m^2) is associated with health problems such as subfertility, osteoporosis, and heart failure.

WEIGHT REDUCTION REDUCES THE RISK OF OSTEOARTHRITIS

Weight loss has many health benefits. It has been found that the risk of osteoarthritis of the knee increases four-fold in women with a BMI of more than 25 kg/m², and five-fold in men with a BMI of 25 kg/m² or more. Being overweight also increases the risk of osteoarthritis of the fingers, indicating that there is more to the causative mechanism than simple mechanical overloading.

Weight reduction reduces the risk of osteoarthritis. The Framingham Knee Osteoarthritis Study showed that the risk of osteoarthritis of the knee decreases by more than 50 per cent for every 5 kg weight loss. In elderly men, a change in BMI category from obese to overweight or overweight to normal reduces the risk of osteoarthritis by 21.5 per cent. In elderly women, a similar change in BMI reduces the risk by 33 per cent.

PRINCIPLES OF WEIGHT LOSS

The Changi Sports Medicine Centre and the Singapore Sports Medicine Centre have collectively helped more that 2,000 patients lose weight effectively and safely through an evidence-based, integrated, multidisciplinary programme. Those who have gone through the programme end up leaner, fitter, and with better control or elimination of their chronic medical conditions. A fuller treatment on the topic of weight management can be found in *Fight the Fat: What You Must Know and Do to Lose Weight* (Ben Tan, published by Marshall Cavendish Editions, 2007), upon which the two Centres have based their weight management programmes. In this chapter, we shall review the principles and pillars that the programme is based on, and deal with aspects of weight management that is specific to runners.

Principle 1: The Need for an Energy Deficit

In order to remove excess body fat, one must incur an energy deficit by burning more energy than what we consume. The body will tap into its energy stores only when there is an energy deficit, and it does so in order to make up for the deficit. For example, if we consume 2,000 kcal and expend 3,000 kcal, the body will first burn up the 2,000 kcal worth of food, and when that is depleted, it then burns body fat to get the additional 1,000 kcal. When we incur an energy deficit, it is natural to feel hungry and lethargic.

If we wish to maintain our weight, then our energy intake should match our expenditure, so that the fat stores will not be touched. If we consume more energy than what we expend, the excess will be stored as fat.

Principle 2: Consistently Incurring and Energy Deficit Leads to Fat Loss

If we incur an energy deficit of 1,000 kcal per day, after a week we would have accumulated a total deficit of 7,000 kcal, and would have burnt and shed 7,000 kcal worth of body fat. This is equivalent to 0.9 kg of body fat!

1 kg of body fat yields 7,700 kcal

Principle 3: The Energy Deficit Needs to be Appropriate

How much energy deficit should we aim for daily? For weight loss, the American College of Sports Medicine recommends a daily energy deficit of 500 – 1,000 kcal. A deficit of 1,000 kcal would result in a weight loss of almost 1 kg per week. This is tempting, but unfortunately it would not be practical for competitive runners as such a deficit will compromise training quality, recovery, adaptation, and immune response. The runner will be prone to injuries and infections.

What happens if we incur an energy deficit in excess of 1,000 kcal? There is a limit to how quickly the fat stores can be released, and this is around 1 kg per week. The greater the energy deficit, the faster the fat release, up to this maximal rate. Beyond this, the body has to look for other sources of energy, and the next source would be protein, mostly from our muscles. Hence, an excessive energy deficit will result not only in fat loss, but also muscle loss. Losing muscle is not wise, as it may result in a lower running economy.

Just as the thermostat of an air conditioner maintains the room at a set temperature, our body has a 'lipostat' that triggers the body into an energy conservation mode whenever it incurs an energy deficit in an attempt to restore the body back to its set weight. If you were to incur a deficit of 200 kcal for example, the body can conserve 200 kcal by slowing your metabolism down, and you end up not losing weight at all. The body is capable of conserving as much as 500 kcal per day, making it difficult to achieve any significant weight loss if we were to incur smaller deficits. Hence, 500 kcal would be an appropriate energy deficit for competitive runners who wish to lose weight without compromising their performance excessively.

The Three Pillars

To achieve the targeted energy deficit, say 500 kcal, an effective, sustainable, and safe way is to reduce the caloric intake and increase the energy expenditure concurrently, as shown in figure 7.1.

Energy intake is reduced through **dietary restriction**, while energy expenditure is increased through both **discretionary exercise** (e.g. running) and **incidental daily activities** (e.g. doing housework). Dietary restriction, discretionary exercise, and incidental daily activities together form the **three pillars** of weight loss. Underlying these three pillars is the behavioural modification that will lead to sustainable weight loss results.

Figure 7.1. The three pillars of weight loss.

YOUR IDEAL WEIGHT FOR DISTANCE RUNNING

There is no doubt that elite distance runners have to be lean, but not all of us can look like a Kenyan runner, with 5 per cent body fat and slender limbs with calves that taper narrowly towards the ankles. The latter ensures that there is minimal mass at the end of the limbs, thus improving running economy. The former not only minimizes the dead weight that the runner carries during the race, but it also maximizes the surface area to volume ratio, thereby improving heat dissipation.

A minority of us are born with, and share the ectomorphic body type (tall, thin and very lean) of the Kenyan runners; while the majority will be mesomorphs (muscular build) or endomorphs (short, plump, and roundish). The latter categories do not exclude you from running as a sport, although they do limit your potential as a top distance runner. However, many of us run half or full marathons not to win the race, but to challenge ourselves to reach our individual potentials. An endomorph cannot become an ectomorph no matter how much weight he loses, but he would be able to run faster than if he had not shed any weight.

For general health, the ideal body mass index [BMI = (Weight in kg) ÷ (Height in m)^2] is 18.5 – 23.0 kg/m^2 for Asians and 18.5 – 25.0 kg/m^2 for Caucasians. Weight loss beyond a BMI of 18.5 kg/m^2 tend to result in excessive loss of muscle and even bone mass, and in extreme cases irregular heart rhythms as well as menstrual disturbances and subfertility in women. For optimal running performance, while lighter is better, there is a limit to how much weight you should lose — crossing this line compromises your running performance. This line varies between individuals, and a way to identify it is by looking at your performance — if you have gone too far and lost too much weight, your running times start to deteriorate rather than improve. To improve on your previous times, your body needs to be healthy and in optimal shape. So if you are looking 'gaunt' but are clocking great times and feeling great, then you probably have nothing to worry about. On the flip side, if your times are deteriorating, then you have probably lost more weight than you should.

WEIGHT LOSS PRESCRIPTION FOR DISTANCE RUNNERS

One approach to weight loss is to eat as little as one reasonably can, and to exercise as much as one reasonably can. Such 'guesstimates' are usually ineffective because the majority of individuals underestimate what they need to do. If our estimates are off the mark, we either lose too much weight too quickly with a resultant drop in running performance or, more commonly, we fail to lose weight at all. By being more precise about the dietary restriction and physical activity that is needed to achieve weight loss, we can then set firm targets and make concrete plans to take action.

Daily Energy Deficit

To lose weight, the runner will need to sustain an energy deficit. Earlier, a deficit of 500 kcal per day was recommended. For a start, you can aim to achieve this deficit, and monitor your weight and running performance over a few weeks. If you fail to lose weight, increase the deficit; if your running performance worsens, then aim for a smaller deficit. To illustrate the individualised energy prescriptions for weight loss, we shall assume that you are aiming for a deficit of 500 kcal per day, i.e.:

$$\text{Energy Expenditure} - \text{Energy Intake} = 500 \text{ kcal}$$

Daily Energy Expenditure

Your energy expenditure is the sum of your resting metabolic rate (RMR), energy expended from incidental daily activities, and energy expended from running and other physical activities.

Your RMR is best determined using a metabolic cart that is available at some sports medicine centres or exercise physiology labs (see figure 6.1, page 97). If you do not have access to this, you can get an estimate by computing your RMR from your body weight:

$$\text{BMR (in kcal/day)} = \text{Body Mass (in kg)} \times 24 \times 1.05$$

Alternatively, the Harris Benedict equation factors in gender and age as well, and would give a more precise estimate:

For males, BMR = 66 + (13.8 x Wt in kg) + (5 x Ht in cm) – (6.8 x Age in years)
For Females, BMR = 655 + (9.6 x Wt in kg) + (1.8 x Ht in cm) – (4.7 x Age in years)

The BMR is the energy expended while at rest. To account for the energy expended through incidental daily activities (e.g. going to work, activities at work), we multiply the BMR by an activity factor to derive your baseline energy expenditure (excluding exercise), BEE. Use a factor of 1.2 if you have a typical office job, and a factor of 1.4 if your job is rather physical (e.g. nurse, physical education teacher):

Sedentary job: BEE = BMR x 1.2
Physical job: BEE = BMR x 1.4

Your total daily energy expenditure (TEE) is the sum of your BEE and the energy expended during discretionary physical activities (PA) such as running. This can be determined from the exercise ergometers (e.g. treadmill, elliptical trainer, cycling ergometer, rowing ergometer) or estimated from exercise tables (e.g. using physical activity calculators available at www.myhealth.sg). Another convenient way is to use a heart rate monitor that has got calorie functions. Hence:

TEE = BEE + PA

Determining Your Appropriate Caloric Intake

The earlier chapters prescribe running programmes to help you improve. That determines your PA, and fixes one end of the energy equation. Assuming that you are aiming for a daily energy deficit of 500 kcal, then:

TEE – Energy Intake = 500, or
Energy Intake = TEE - 500

As an illustration, let us take a 75-kg runner with a BMI of 26 kg/m², working as an accountant and running 50 km per week at an average pace of 10 km/h. From his running programme, he would expend 3,850 kcal per week and that averages out to 550 kcal per day (a 75 kg runner burns 770 kcal per hour when running at 10 km/h). His BMR would be 75 x 24 x 1.05 = 1,890 kcal per day. Given that he has a sedentary job, his BEE would be 1,890 x 1.2 = 2,268 kcal per day. That would give him a total a TEE of 2,268 + 550 = 2,818 kcal per day. To lose weight while having adequate energy to put in a quality training programme, he will have to limit his dietary intake to 2,818 – 500 = 2,300 kcal per day.

Monitoring Your Progress

As the computations are based on estimates, the caloric intake will need to be adjusted based on the weight loss progress and running performance. If no weight loss is evident after two weeks, then adjust the intake downwards by 100 kcal until there is a measurable weight loss.

To monitor progress, the weight should be recorded and charted weekly. A reliable way to measure body weight is to do so in the morning, after emptying the bladder and bowel, before consuming any food or fluids.

Running performance should be monitored as well. Keep track of training times in your training diary and be on the lookout for any deterioration. For example, if you were comfortably clocking 60 minutes for your 10 km base runs, and you now find yourself struggling to match that time, then consider letting up on the diet a little.

Timing

It is difficult to endure an energy deficit and perform optimally at the same time. Hence, weight loss should be attempted at opportune times during your training cycles. A good time would be at the start of your training cycle, when the targeted race is several weeks away. As you step up your training towards your peak, you will need the energy to sustain the high mileage and training intensities, as well as to recover from your training bouts and stave of infections. For these reasons, it is a good idea to avoid incurring an energy deficit as you peak and taper for a race.

Another opportunity to lose weight is during the transition phase (i.e. after a peak and before the start of the next training cycle). Most runners take a month's break after a major marathon before resuming their training, and this would be a good time to lose weight. However, commence the planned dietary restriction only five days or more after the marathon to give adequate time for recovery and repair.

HEALTHY DIETARY RESTRICTION
Which Diet?

There are numerous diets available, e.g. Atkin's diet, the Zone diet, the South Beach Diet, Eat Right for Your Type (advocating different diets for different blood groups), Volumetrics, the Ornish Diet, and the Pritikin Diet. They may be very low fat (e.g. Ornish and Pritikin diets), low carbohydrate (e.g. Atkins diet), high protein (e.g. The Zone Diet), or take a balanced approach. Some have sound philosophies, while others are questionable.

Do these diets help you lose weight? Probably, and the reason is simple. All diet plans impose rules on what you can or cannot eat. These rules place restrictions on the individual, and by adhering to these various diet plans rather than eating as he or she wishes, the individual eats less than usual. To put it simply, these diets induce weight loss ultimately through a reduction in caloric intake, whatever the philosophy behind the diet plan.

The real question is whether the diet helps you lose weight without compromising your performance. Low carbohydrate diets are out — slow runs are still possible while on low carbohydrate diets, but you will have difficulty with higher training intensities such as tempo runs. High fat, low carbohydrate diets are thought to train the body to better metabolise fat as a fuel source, but it is the stored fat that we want the body to mobilise, not the ingested fat — we certainly are not going to ingest fat during the race as it will delay gastric emptying and impair water absorption. High protein diets aid repair and recovery, but repair requires the energy from carbohydrates as well, so the protein should be accompanied with carbohydrates. Very low calorie diets (< 800 kcal per day) result in not only fat loss, but also muscle loss, but we need our muscles to run well. That leaves the runner looking to cut weight with only one safe option — a moderate, well-balanced diet.

Ensure a Balanced and Wholesome Diet

After working out your energy intake target, the next step is to plan a diet that meets the prescribed energy intake. To do this, we need to know the calorie content of various micronutrients:

1 g fat	= 9 kcal or 37 kJ
1 g carbohydrate	= 4 kcal or 16 kJ
1 g protein	= 4 kcal or 17 kJ
1 g alcohol	= 7 kcal or 29 kJ

Because of the high energy density of fat, reducing your fat intake is an effective way of reducing the total caloric intake. Try to keep your fat intake well below 30 per cent of your total energy intake.

Human physiology is very complex, and our bodies require a whole range of macronutrients and micronutrients to function optimally. Hence, it is not good to cut out any nutrient totally, including fat. Ensure that you have a good mix of various macronutrients, and that your carbohydrate and protein needs are met as discussed in Chapter 6.

Our bodies are quite smart (it needs to be, otherwise we would not be around today), and if any major nutrient is lacking, we develop a specific craving for it. For example, those who have been on the Atkins diet will attest to cravings for carbohydrates. Cravings make it difficult to adhere to our diets, and a balanced diet minimizes cravings.

The total daily caloric intake should be evenly distributed throughout the day, e.g. three regular meals a day plus a small post-training snack. Meals should be just heavy enough such that you do not need to snack in between meals. Skipping meals is a bad idea as it makes you so hungry that at the next meal, you will tend to over-eat and exceed your calorie quota for the day.

Monitoring Your Intake

A good way to ensure that you are indeed adhering to your prescribed energy intake is to keep a food diary. Once a week, record what you eat after each meal (rather than by recall at the end of the day), and at the end of the day, convert it to calories and add up the total energy intake for the day. Nutrition calculators are available on many websites, including www.myhealth.sg.

"Weighing in at 84 kg and at a height of 1.7 m, I was obese as a teenager. I decided that this would change after I started to gain mass again after my national service. I would tire out easily and there was always a sense of lethargy. I decided to take up running in 2005, partly to maintain my weight loss, and eventually, I ran for the love of the sport and keeping my weight down became an effortless by-product of my running. I now weigh 63 kg and feel so light on my feet. Not only do I feel better, I am also happy with my running performance."

– Dr Benny Goh, winner of the 2009 Adidas Sundown Marathon (84km) in a course record time of 7:36:05. His marathon personal best time is 2:52.

08. RACE STRATEGY

>>With input from M Rameshon & G Elangovan

In the earlier chapters, you learnt how to optimise training, nutrition and technique to improve running performance. Having worked hard during the preparation phase to prime your body for peak performance, the next step is to perform well during the race itself. Often, you hear of runners who put in a whole year of sweat, only to pull out of the marathon race at the 35 km mark because of severe cramps, or running out of steam towards the end of the race and finishing in a time that is worse than that during training because they started out too fast.

Compared to most other sports, race strategy in marathon running is simple — the challenge is in sticking to it. In this chapter, we will learn how to draw up and execute a sound race plan, so that all your preparation translates to results that you will be pleased with.

RACE PACE

The crux of the marathon race strategy is the race pace. There is an optimal pace for each runner. Too conservative a pace, and you finish the race with too much in reserve and kick yourself for not pushing harder. More commonly, runners aim for too fast a pace and run out of steam, finishing badly or not even finishing at all. Picking the right race pace is a gamble — do you go for a faster pace than your previous marathon, and if you do, how much faster? What we want to do is to take a calculated risk, rather than arbitrarily coming up with a figure.

Determining the Race Pace

Your targeted finishing time, and hence your average race pace, can be determined from:

- **Previous marathon time.** Naturally, every runner wants to be faster, so assuming the course is of similar difficulty, aim to be slightly faster. Cutting 15 minutes off the previous marathon time of four hours flat is reasonable, but to cut 15 minutes off a previous time of 3:15 hrs is a stretch.

- **Time trials.** If you do not have a recent marathon time to go by, then do some time trials to determine what your race pace should be. A convenient guide to go by is to double your half marathon time plus 10 minutes, e.g. if your half marathon time is two hours flat, then your targeted marathon time should be (2 x 2 hr) + 10 min = 4:10 hrs.

From the projected time, make adjustments for the course, weather, and crowd conditions. Often, the difference between a tropical and a temperate marathon is around five to 10 minutes.

Once you have set a targeted finishing time, work out the average race pace that you have to maintain. For example, if you are aiming to finish the marathon in four hours flat, then your race pace should be (4 x 60) ÷ 42.195 = 5:41 min/km.

Pacing within the Race

During the marathon, the pace may vary at different stretches of the course. Assuming a flat course with a constant temperature throughout, there are two pacing strategies that you can adopt:

- **Even pace.** This is the safest and best-accepted strategy.
- **Negative split.** You can split the marathon into four 10 km stretches or two 21 km stretches. The latter is more common. A negative split is when the later stretch is run in a shorter time than the earlier stretch.

Aiming and planning to run the first half much faster than the second half of a marathon is suicidal — during the race, your second half will likely be much slower than you had planned for, so do not do this unless there are exceptional reasons. Many inexperienced runners make this mistake inadvertently.

Marathon world records are set using an even pace or with a very slight negative split. The best runners in the world run their races with the time for each kilometre within an extremely tight range that is only a few seconds apart.

Sticking to the Race Pace

During the race, there will be many factors that will throw the runner off his pace, including crowded conditions, hills, congested drink stations, dehydration, the urge to go to the toilet, weather conditions, niggling injuries (e.g. abrasions, blisters), stitches, hitting the wall, and loss of concentration. Most of these factors slow the runner down, but there are occasionally factors that make the runner go too fast, e.g. feeling strong, downhill course (the Boston Marathon, for instance, starts with a long downhill stretch that tires out the hamstrings of unwary runners), sticking with neighbouring runners that are going too fast.

Every runner will feel good at the start of the race, as he or she is undoubtedly feeling fresh. But the real race does not start till the last 10 km, and the runner needs to have enough in reserve for this last stretch, when his or her carbohydrate stores are near empty.

To stick to the race pace, here is what you need to do:

1. Decide on your average race pace, preferably in minutes per kilometre.
2. Work out the expected elapsed time at each kilometre (or at intervals where there are distance markers, depending on the race organisation), if you were to hold an even pace. There are 'pace calculators' on the Internet that will make this task easier.

MEET SINGAPORE'S ULTRA-MAN

When he tried out for the Naval Diving Unit, Kua Harn Wei almost drowned. The near-death experience spurred him to learn how to swim and now, the Assistant Professor at NUS is an ultra-triathlete with an Ironman personal best of 10 hr 49 min, set in 2003. A single Ironman comprises a 3.8-km swim, 180-km cycling and 42.2-km run.

Harn Wei has progressed to do Deca Ironmans, i.e. he does one Ironman a day for 10 days in a row! As if running one marathon a day for 10 consecutive days is not challenging enough, Harn Wei also swims 3,800 km and cycles 18,000 km during those 10 days. To top it off, in 2008, Harn Wei was ranked world number two in the Ultra Triathlon World Cup!

For marathoners who are struggling in the last 10 km (that's practically all of us), Harn Wei advises, "In order to participate and complete a race, you need to be sensitive to your body and listen to what it is telling you. With experience, through training and competing, you learn how to accurately interpret what your body is trying to tell you. Not all unpleasant sensations spell doom. Say, you start to feel an unfamiliar strain 10 km from the finish of a marathon. The natural reaction is to panic and think, 'This is not my day! Perhaps I should quit.' Do not panic — do whatever you can to solve the problem. For example, adjust your running gait slightly, or slow the pace down a little. Don't expect everything to be smooth sailing — be prepared for the unexpected (such as high temperatures, missing a water station, or even mistaking the sports drink for water and pouring it over your head) and problem-solve along the way."

3. Carry this with you during the race, either by (a) writing it down on your forearm with indelible ink on the morning of the race, (b) printing it out on paper, laminating it, and loosely strapping it onto your wrist as a wrist band, or (c) laminating it and carrying it in your pocket.

4. You will need a light watch with a clear digital display, as you will be checking the time on the run.

You might think it would be easier to do the math along the way or to memorise elapsed times, but during a long race, your mind will not be as dependable as you expect.

Here are more tips on keeping to your race pace:

- Include pace runs during training to get a feel of the race pace — experienced runners can keep accurately to the race pace even without looking at their watches.

VIVIAN TANG

Singapore's fastest female marathoner, is known for her consistent pacing and negative splits. "For me, I always run at my own pace. Many run off very fast in the first couple of kilometres but I'll make sure I check my watch for the first 2 or 3 km. I know its a long race so if my competitor is ahead of me, that's ok. I'll try to catch her later if possible. If not, I know she's a better runner," says Vivian. Her personal best of 2:56:27 was set at the 2008 Singapore Marathon, where she ran the first 21 km in 1:28:14 and the second half in 1:28.13! In that race, Vivian was not distracted by her closest Singaporean rival, who ran a blistering 2:50 marathon just two months earlier. "We were in the same running pack for one to two kilometres at the start," said Vivian. "After that, she disappeared!" Vivian passed her at the 21 km mark.

- Pre-arrange to run the race together with an experienced runner whom you know will be running at your desired pace. Preferably, train together prior to the race so that you are familiar with each other's pacing abilities and habits. Start together and during the race, cooperate and help each other maintain pace.

- Practice drinking on the run — do not slow down more than necessary.

- Start the race in the corral that corresponds to your planned finishing time. In some races, organizers do not strictly enforce this and slower runners may crowd the corrals nearer the starting line. Arrive at your corral early in order not to be displaced by these runners.

- During the race, the natural tendency is to go with the flow and keep pace with the runners around you. If those around you were aiming for the same pace, then that would help. But if their plan is different from yours, they will throw you off your pace. Hence, I like to go for marathon races with running buddies who are of the same pace as me, so we can help one another keep pace.

- Some marathon organisers provide pacers — these are usually experienced runners who can accurately hold pace. Follow them if their pace is the same as yours.

- Hold back for at least the first 10 – 21 km — do not get too far ahead of the planned pace. Do not be too pleased if you see yourself 20 minutes ahead of schedule early on in the race — it only spells trouble later on.

- The last 10 or more kilometres is where the race plan is likely to fall apart. To maintain your concentration for the last 10 km, hydrate and refuel along the way, rather than waiting till the last 10 km to do this.

The toughest part of the race is the last 10 km — often, your body will move only at its own pace and will not listen to you when you will it to move faster. Apart from training harder to become fitter, mental strength is critical. It certainly helps to use positive imagery (e.g. visualizing yourself successfully crossing the finishing line) and process thinking (using key phrases to focus your mind and body on the task at hand) to keep you on track and focused. For example, to prevent the deterioration of running form and hence running economy that occurs with fatigue, I repeat the keyword 'rebound' (to remind myself to generate and take advantage of the rebound from each step) to myself and visualise Samuel Wanjiru's (2008 Beijing Olympic Marathon men's gold medallist) running style, to get my body to conform to the optimal running gait.

It is natural for negative thoughts to creep into your mind, for example, "Why don't I just give up?" or, "I hate this!" Displace such thoughts with positive imagery and positive self-talk, such as, "Wow, what a ride!" or "This is what I've been waiting for!" Avoid using negative terms during self-talk, such as "Don't slow down." Instead, tell yourself, "Keep it up." Both have the same meaning, but by using the phrase "slow down," the image is brought up in your mind and you may actually do it, even if it is preceded by the term "don't." Here's an illustration: "Don't think about how sour a lemon is." Did the thought of a sour lemon cause you to salivate?

> "The most important aspect of race strategy is to have faith in yourself. That is, to trust in the work that you've done to build up for the big day, to stick to the pacing that you've ground into your legs over all those training miles, to believe that following your own beat will take you to your goal - whether it is to win, to set a personal best, or just to finish."
>
> — Jeanette Wang, two-time Sundown Ultramarathon champion
> and one of Singapore's top Ironman

DRAFTING

Race cars do it, road bikes do it, and runners can do it too! Runners encounter air resistance as they run, and this expends energy. Air resistance increases with running speed, headwind, and air density (air is denser in colder environments). By running closely behind another runner and using the front runner as a shield, we can save some energy. This is termed drafting.

Drafting is certainly beneficial in race cars and road bikes, but less so in running. The energy saved is thought to be significant only when running above an estimated threshold speed of 18 km/h or in a strong headwind. There is also a beneficial psychological effect — it is mentally easier to 'hang on' to the runner in front than to be the breakaway runner. But do weigh the benefits against the disadvantages, such as the risk of running into the runner in front and the feeling of being closed-in when running inside a pack.

To take advantage of the front runner's slipstream, run directly behind, as close as you can comfortably get. If there the wind is blowing from the side, then run behind and to the downwind side to stay in the person's wind shadow.

MARATHON PRE-RACE CHECKLIST

You have prepared long and hard for your marathon, and you do not want anything to go wrong just before or during the race. Do not leave anything to chance. Do not try anything unfamiliar. Go through the checklist below to ensure that 'unexpected' mishaps do not occur.

As soon as they are ready, check the race details (from the race website and, once you collect it, the race pack). Key information that you will need include the start time (there may be different start times for different categories), course map and terrain, site maps for the starting and finish areas, intervals between distance markers, brand of sports drink provided, locations of the drink stations, expected weather, how to get there, and traffic information (e.g. road closures, parking).

☑ Do reconnaissance runs at least a few days before the marathon to familiarise with the course, especially the challenging stretches. Do visualisation exercises to mentally prepare for these stretches.

☑ From the start time, work backwards to decide what time you need to wake up, making allowance for traffic, parking, bag deposit, toilet trips (expect long queues), crowds at the starting corrals, stretching, and warm up. Get accustomed to waking up at this time a day or two before the race.

☑ Taper five to 14 days before the race.

☑ Carbo-load and hydrate two to three days before the race.

☑ Collect your race pack early and check race website for last minute updates.

☑ Memorise where the drink and gel stations are located. Plan the points at which you will consume your carbohydrate gels.

☑ Visualise the route.

☑ Due to pre-race jitters, runners may not sleep well the night before the race. Hence, two nights before the race, ensure that you have adequate sleep.

☑ The day before the race, pin on your number tag, attach the timing chip, and set aside your running apparel and shoes. Prepare your gel packs and place them in your shorts pockets. Prepare your pacing schedule. Set your alarm clock. Get your friends who are doing the same race (or the hotel if you are overseas) to give you a wake up call as a back up. Check the latest weather updates.

☑ Sleep early, but not too early or you may have difficulty falling asleep.

☑ On race day, once you wake up, have a light breakfast and consume fluids. Empty bladder and bowel. Shower if that is your practice, and gear up. Write your pacing schedule on your forearm or put on your pacing band.

☑ On arrival, apply Vaseline to prevent any chafing, deposit your bag, empty your bladder again, and make your way to the starting corral. Warm up and stretch in or near the corral.

☑ While waiting for the start, go through your race plan in your mind. Remember not to start out too fast and hydrate and refuel along the way.

Just a last note before you launch off the starting line. Marathons are mass events with big crowds. To make it enjoyable for yourself and fellow runners, do observe race etiquette (see appendix 3).

HANG IN THERE!

Khoo Swee Chiow, Singapore's most prominent adventurer, has climbed Mt Everest twice, skied to the South & North Poles, climbed the Seven Summits (the seven highest peaks in the seven continents), and swum across the 39-km Malacca Straits. Swee Chiow also holds two Guinness World Records for the Longest Scuba Submergence of 220 hours and Longest Journey on Skates, 6,088 km from Hanoi to Singapore.

Swee Chiow shares with us what keeps him going, "In endurance events, it's always mind over matter. When the going gets tough, I look for reasons to justify the pain in order to carry on. I tell myself,

Pain is temporary — As long I won't die or suffer serious permanent injury, I can keep going. If I really can't run, I will walk but I won't stop. The storm won't last forever. The wind will stop and the sun will shine again. I just got to hang in there for a while.

Memory playback — If I can climb Mt Everest, ski to South and North Pole, surely I can do this. I also playback the positive memories from those trips e.g. the fabulous sunrise and sunset at high altitude and the view from the top of the world.

Hard work endured — The months of preparations will be wasted if I quit now.

Loved ones waiting — My family is waiting for me at home. Let's just get on with it and complete the task. The sooner I finish the challenge, the sooner I can be home.

Leaving a legacy — If I quit, what lesson am I teaching my two kids? What example am I showing them?"

TIPS FROM THE TOP

- Countdown to race day — Pin up a countdown chart from 100 days to Race Day on your fridge door

- Make the necessary sacrifices — Plan your long run sessions early Sunday morning and avoid late Saturday nights

- Motivate yourself — Find that something that will make you tick. For example, whenever you feel de-motivated, go grab a *Runners' World* magazine. It will help you refocus and make you want to run the next minute

- Route visualization — Drive through the race route or train on some section of the route. Go through the route in your mind before sleeping

- Prepare for the unexpected — Always have a plan 'B'. For example, if you fall sick during your preparation phase, take a break and substitute that week with your unloading week

- Break your race into bite sizes — At the start line don't worry about the finish. Instead, think about reaching the 10 km mark smiling, the 20 km mark waving to your family and friends, the 30 km mark showing thumbs up signs, and finally at the 42 km mark, start laughing through the last 195 m

- What to do after the race — Whatever the result, plan for a short getaway. Appreciate and celebrate the entire process — rather than the result — that you took to get to the finishing line

G. Elangovan
Three-time winner of the Singapore Marathon

♥ 09. STAYING INJURY-FREE

>>With input from Adele Ang, Shamsynar Ani, Jason Chia, Naomi Chua, Sharon Khoo, Darek Lam, Fabian Lim, Jessie Phua & Roger Tian

Injuries are any athlete's worst nightmare. The harder we train, the faster we improve, but there is a point of diminishing returns or 'injury threshold' (see figure 9.1). Beyond this threshold, our performance drops, we suffer a series of overuse injuries, and put ourselves at risk of the dreaded overtraining syndrome.

The point of diminishing returns varies greatly between individuals — there are runners like Paul Tergat who hit 300 km per week without injury, while others get stress fractures at 20 km per week. This threshold also

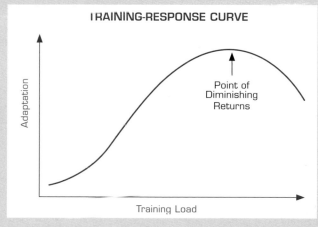

Figure. 9.1. As training load increases, so does training adaptation, up to the point of diminishing returns.

varies within the same individual during different phases of his or her running career. To discover this point, we push ourselves to the boundaries, and sometimes, it takes an injury to occur before we find that point. Runners therefore need a good feel of their bodies, to sense the onset of injury even before it happens and to recognise the early signs of injury and manage them quickly. Early recognition and prompt management reduces downtime.

Besides training errors, which account for 60 per cent of running injuries, factors such as faulty equipment (e.g. worn-out shoes), excessive body weight, abnormal biomechanics (e.g. overpronation, ankle stiffness) or anatomy (e.g. malalignment), muscle tightness and weakness also affect this threshold and increases the risk of injury.

Running is a high impact sport — depending on speed, terrain and footwear, the ground reaction force (GRF) generated during heel strike can range between one and a half to five times of body weight. Grass exerts a dampening effect on the GRF, whereas downhill running increases it substantially. The muscles, tendons, joints and bones of the lower extremity bear the brunt of this impact. Hence, it is not surprising that more than two-thirds of injuries affect this region.

It is important to identify the root cause or causes of running injuries, so that they may be addressed. Otherwise, recurrences tend to occur. Apart from identifying and addressing root causes, the management of the injured runner also involves symptom relief and avoiding further damage to the injured tissue. Rehabilitation and physiotherapy is often required to promote healing and correct muscle imbalances.

Prevention is better than cure; hence, all runners should adopt good habits such as gradual mileage increments, regular footwear inspection for signs of wear and tear, and follow a flexibility and conditioning program to ensure that they are "fit to run". Pain or discomfort is a warning that something is amiss, and runners should learn to listen to their bodies and heed these signs.

OVERTRAINING SYNDROME

Overtraining syndrome occurs when an athlete is training intensely over an extended period. But instead of improving, he shows deterioration in performance, even after resting for more than two weeks. About 70 per cent of high-level endurance athletes have experienced (or will experience) overtraining during their career. The signs and symptoms to watch out for are:

- Increased resting heart rate (measured in the morning before getting up from bed). An increase of more than six to 10 beats per minute is significant
- Loss of appetite
- Loss of weight
- Sleep disturbance
- Emotional instability (anger, anxiety, irritability, depression, apathy, poor concentration)
- Early fatigue
- Frequent and prolonged infections

Tipping yourself over into overtraining syndrome is a costly mistake to make, as the downtime needed to snap out of it usually takes more than two weeks. To get out of it quickly, stop running, cross train, sleep adequately, and eat well.

COMMON RUNNING INJURIES

Every year, between 25 – 70 per cent of runners sustain an injury that affects their training. However, serious problems are rare, and injury rates remain two to six times lower than sports such as cycling, soccer and skiing. The common sites of injuries in runners are listed in figure 9.2.

COMMON SITES OF INJURIES IN RUNNERS

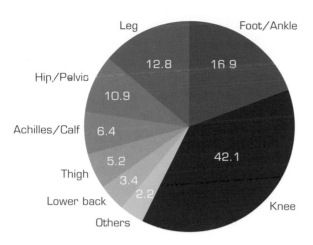

Figure 9.2. Injury sites and their respective frequencies (per cent) in 2,002 runners. Source: Taunton JE et al., A retrospective case-control analysis of 2,002 running injuries. British Journal of Sports Medicine 2002; 36: 95-101

Common injuries include the patellofemoral pain syndrome, iliotibial band friction syndrome, plantar fasciitis, meniscal injuries, Achilles tendon injuries, muscle strains, medial tibial stress syndrome, stress fractures and skin disorders. The following discussion highlights salient points in the more common running injuries, with the aim of raising awareness so that runners can seek help promptly. Understanding the injury mechanisms, as well as the intrinsic and extrinsic factors that lead to the common running injuries is the prerequisite to preventing injuries in the first place. The list is by no means complete. Your sports physician will arrive at a diagnosis and direct the management of your problem with the help of sports physiotherapists, sports trainers, podiatrists, and other clinicians.

Patellofemoral Pain Syndrome

Patellofemoral pain syndrome (PFPS) is the most common injury in distance runners, especially females. It is also known as runner's knee or chondromalacia patellae (CMP). This condition is due to the mal-tracking of the kneecap (patella) within the V-shaped trochlea of the thighbone (femur). The kneecap travels up and down a groove called the trochlea in the lower end of the thighbone. When mal-tracking occurs, the kneecap travels to one side of the groove, like a train with one wheel off the track. This creates excessive friction between the two bones and damages the cartilage lining the patellofemoral joint (see figure 9.3).

This in turn causes pain that is felt diffusely around or under the kneecap. Activities that require the knee to flex, such as running, stairs, squats, prolonged sitting in cramped areas such as cinemas or aircraft, are often painful. This may be associated with a crackling sensation or sound (crepitus).

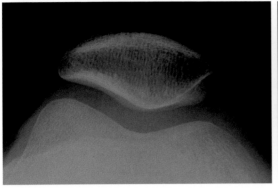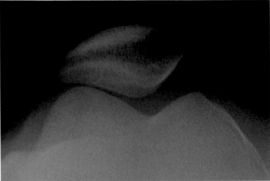

Figure 9.3. The kneecap sitting on the trochlea (groove) of the femur. The X-ray on the left shows a centrally tracking kneecap. The X-ray on the right shows a malaligned kneecap that is displaced and tilted towards the outside (lateral aspect) of the knee.

The patellofemoral joint experiences great compressive force — three times body weight when running on level ground, two and a half times climbing up stairs, three and a half times going down stairs, and seven and a half times squatting with knees bent at 90°. These forces are even more intense when there is mal-tracking. In cases of mal-tracking, the patella is almost always displaced laterally (towards the outside of the knee), due to the lateral pull from a tight iliotibial band (ITB) and the muscles attached to it (e.g. outer quadriceps and hamstrings, gluteus medius, gluteus maximus), with the medially-placed vastus medialis oblique (VMO) muscle unable to counteract the pull adequately. Anatomical and biomechanical factors such as wide hips, overpronation and flat feet (pes planus) can also alter patella tracking.

PFPS can be painful, but in the early stages, it is not a serious condition as the pain is due to frictional/compression forces and there is no structural damage. If left unmanaged, the cartilage in the patellofemoral joint wears off irreversibly, leading to even more severe pain and joint swelling. Hence, PFPS and the factors that contribute to mal-tracking should be addressed before structural damage occurs, necessitating more invasive treatment options.

Your sports physiotherapist will teach you how to stretch your ITBs (see figure 9.4), perform soft tissue massage for the muscles attached to the ITB, and supervise strengthening of your VMOs. Other contributing factors need to be identified and addressed as well. During the four to six weeks that is usually required to correct the muscle imbalance, you may wish to substitute one or two sessions of running with lower impact activities such as the elliptical trainer, front-crawl swimming or cycling. The use of sports tape to aid patella tracking and pain perception can also provide a temporary symptom relief during training.

Figure 9.4. An example of an ITB stretch for the left hip and thigh.

Figure 9.5. The iliotibial band (ITB) rubs over the lateral femoral epicondyle and greater trochanter.

Labels in Figure 9.5: Iliotibial Band, Greater Trochanter, Lateral Femoral Epicondyle

Iliotibial Band Friction Syndrome

The iliotibial band (ITB) is a thick, fibrous band of tissue that runs from the hip, down the outer part of the thigh, and is attached to the tibia (shin bone) (see figure 9.5). When standing upright, it lies in front of a sharp prominence (lateral femoral epicondyle) on the femur. When the knee is alternately flexed and extended, as in running, the ITB moves back and forth across this prominence. Friction is thus generated and is maximal at 20° – 30° of flexion.

If there is too much friction, such as in those with tight ITBs, weak hip abductors, high mileages, iliotibial band friction syndrome (ITBFS) might occur, marked by localised inflammation and tenderness. Pain is felt on the outside of the knee, typically after reaching a certain threshold mileage. Less commonly, the frictional pain may instead be felt where the ITB crosses the bony prominence on the side of the hip joint called the greater trochanter. The pain intensifies as the athlete continues running, and may be severe enough to stop a runner from finishing the half or full marathon. Downhill running worsens symptoms, whereas sprinting and level ground running is less painful.

Pain relief can be achieved through the use of anti-inflammatory medication or ice. When severe, your sports physician can deliver a localised cortisone injection to relieve the inflammation. The ITB and its attached muscles should be stretched daily, accompanied by soft tissue massage, to reduce the friction between the ITB and the lateral femoral epicondyle or greater trochanter. Those with weak hip abductors need to strengthen them. During long runs, stop to stretch the ITB (see figure 9.4) prior to the threshold distance, before continuing again. Surgical release or lengthening of the ITB is reserved for recalcitrant cases.

Patellar Tendinosis

Repeated impact can result in a traction injury at the junction between the patellar tendon and the kneecap. Micro-tears of the tendon-bone junction accumulate to form a degenerative lesion that is tender when the inferior pole of the kneecap is touched (see figure 9.6). The higher the cumulative impact, the higher the risk. Those who are overweight, have weak quadricep muscles, have high medial longitudinal arches in the feet, train on hard surfaces, or do excessive plyometric training (e.g. bounding) have a tendency to develop

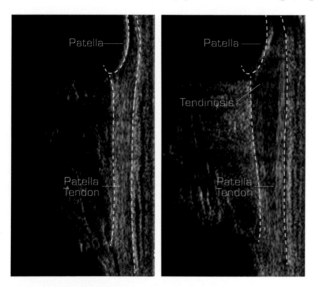

Figure 9.6. Normal patellar tendon (left) and patellar tendinosis (right) in the left and right knee respectively of the same patient. The ultrasound scan on the right shows a dark, triangular lesion just under the kneecap, extending down the patellar tendon.

patellar tendinosis. As the pain is usually tolerable in the early stages, the injury tends to be in its more advanced stages by the time the runner sees a doctor.

Patellar tendinosis tends to be chronic and resistant to treatment. To stimulate the healing process, extra corporeal shockwave therapy (ESWT) may be attempted (see boxed text, page 142), together with cessation of impact activities for six to 12 weeks. Stretches and strengthening of the quadricep muscles improve shock absorption and unloads the tendon-bone junction. Other biomechanical causes such as training drills, training surfaces, shoes, and high medial arches of the feet need to be addressed to further reduce the impact forces.

Meniscal Injuries

The menisci are two pieces of C-shaped fibrocartilage that function as shock absorbers in each knee, protecting the softer articular cartilage covering the femur (see figure 9.7a and 9.7b). Impact forces or sudden pivoting (e.g. side-stepping to avoid an obstacle) when the limb is bearing weight can tear the menisci. Cumulative impact over many years can lead to degenerative tears often seen in middle-aged runners.

The site of pain and tenderness corresponds to the location of the tear, which can be on the inside, outside, or back of the knee. Squatting, twisting, pivoting, or impact activities can cause pain. There may be a mild to moderate swelling of the affected knee.

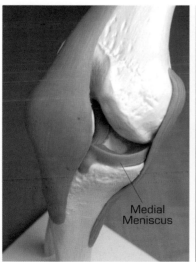
Medial Meniscus

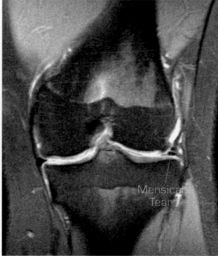
Mensical Tear

Figure 9.7a. (left) Oblique view of the right knee, showing the C-shaped medial meniscus.

Figure 9.7b. (right) Magnetic resonance imaging (MRI) demonstrating a tear through the meniscus. The medial and lateral menisci in the knee serve as shock absorbers. However, medial mensical tears are more common.

Depending on the size, location, and type of tear, some meniscal tears can heal with conservative treatment while others require arthroscopy (keyhole surgery) to either repair or trim off the torn part of the meniscus. Your sports physician will help you differentiate them, with or without a magnetic resonance imaging (MRI) scan, and advice you accordingly. A trial of conservative management includes a four to six week period of minimising all painful and aggravating activities accompanied by physiotherapy and anti-inflammatory medication to manage the knee swelling, if any.

Muscle Soreness and Strains

Mild muscle soreness or a sensation of tightness is common after training, especially after interval training. Short term loading of the muscles beyond what they are accustomed to (i.e. over-reaching) is part and parcel of training and adaptation. The resultant sensation is called delayed-onset muscle soreness (DOMS). This is harmless and is not considered an injury. If your training intensity is just right, then you should feel a slight soreness the next day. If you feel so sore that you have to get out of a chair or go down a flight of stairs gingerly,

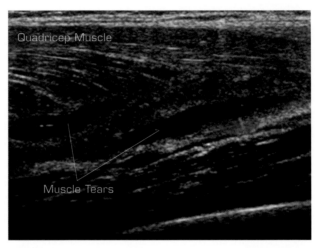

Figure 9.8. Ultrasound scan showing two muscle tears with a collections of blood (haematomas) in the quadriceps of an athlete.

then you have probably overdone it. DOMS usually peaks 48 hours after a hard training session and resolves within five days. Stretching, sports massage, recovery runs, and cross training help to relieve DOMS and enhance recovery.

A muscle strain, on the other hand, is more serious as there is actual muscle damage. A grade 1 strain is where there are microscopic tears in the muscle; grade 2, a small partial tear with minimal gap between the torn edges; and grade 3, an obvious gap with a collection of blood (haematoma). A strain is more localised and sharper than DOMS, and in severe cases, a gap or depression in the muscle may appear or there may be visible bruising near the site of the tear. The pain is usually acute and felt during training, but in milder cases, it may be felt only after training. Common sites for muscle tears or strains are in the calves, hamstrings, quadriceps, and the gluteal muscles. The degree of tenderness or pain may not relate with the severity of the tear, and it is often difficult to grade a tear by physical examination — a quick ultrasound scan by your sports physician confirms the grade so that the appropriate treatment option can be chosen (see figure 9.8).

First aid management for muscle strains comprises the R-I-C-E regime:

- **R**est the injured muscle
- **I**ce for 15 – 20 minutes, three to four times per day
- **C**ompress with a bandage or Turbigrip stocking
- **E**levate the injured limb

Avoid applying heat, vigorous massage, or overzealous stretching, as they will cause more bleeding and damage. Large haematomas may require aspiration under ultrasound guidance. The down time varies from two to six weeks depending on severity. Importantly, muscle flexibility and strength must be restored before returning to full training. Those who simply rest till the pain disappears and return to running without restoring flexibility and strength are inviting a recurrence.

Plantar Fasciitis

The plantar fascia is a tough and fibrous triangular sheet of tissue that runs from the heel bone (calcaneum) to the undersurface of the toes (see figure 9.9). Besides helping to hold up the longitudinal arch of the foot, it also helps in shock absorption and energy conservation. During walking and running, the arch drops around 1 cm after heel strike. This stretches the plantar fascia, which subsequently recoils during push-off, returning up to 80 per cent of the stored energy.

Figure 9.9. The plantar fascia helps hold up the medial arch. When overloaded, the end attached to the heel bone swells up.

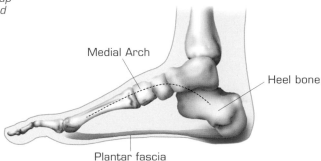

Medial Arch

Heel bone

Plantar fascia

The repeated traction of the plantar fascia on its insertion into the heel bone, if excessive, can result in micro-tears and degeneration, causing swelling and pain (see figure 9.11). Plantar fasciitis is common in those who are overweight, have flat feet or high arches, or spend a lot of time on their feet.

Chronic traction of the plantar fascia on the heel bone may cause a traction spur to develop over time, and hence the name "heel spur." It is noteworthy that the spur is the result — not the cause — of the traction, so its removal does not relieve the traction or the pain significantly.

Pain is experienced at the base of the heel after running or during the first few steps after bed rest or prolonged sitting. Direct pressure onto the plantar fascia insertion (medial calcaneal process) can be exquisitely tender. The normal plantar fascia thickness at the insertion into the heel bone is less than 4 mm (see figure 9.10). In those with plantar fasciitis, an ultrasound scan will show a swollen plantar facia (see figure 9.11). X-rays are not necessary for diagnosis, as the bone spur, if present, is inconsequential.

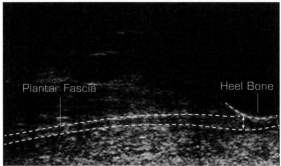
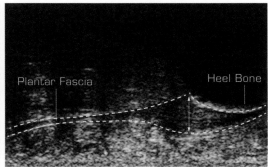

Figure 9.10. Ultrasound scan of a normal fascia, with a thickness of 2.9 mm (arrows)

Figure 9.11. Ultrasound scan of a swollen plantar fascia with a thickness of 6.5 mm (arrows)

The plantar fascia swelling can be relieved with oral anti-inflammatory medication and physiotherapy, cortisone injection, or extra corporeal shockwave therapy (ESWT). For runners, cortisone injection into the plantar fascia is generally avoided, as it increases the risk of a rupture. Concurrently, traction forces within the plantar fascia must be reduced through customised orthotics (with a medial arch support, plantar fascia accommodation, and an aperture for the swollen area) and plantar fascia stretches. If the above are inadequate, taping of the foot offers additional protection.

Achilles Tendon Injuries
The Achilles is the thickest and strongest tendon in the body (see figure 9.12a). It is approximately

37 cm long, and its elastic properties play an important role in energy conservation. The potential energy generated during heel strike is stored in the stretched tendon, which subsequently recoils and returns nearly 35 per cent of this energy during propulsion. Overuse injuries can affect its insertion into the heel bone (enthesiopathy, see figure 9.12b) or approximately 4 – 6 cm above the heel bone (tendinopathy). Those who have excessive weight, forefoot landing, excessive pronation, flat feet or high longitudinal arch, calf tightness, weak calves, and high intensity training are particularly susceptible to Achillies tendon injury.

Figure 9.12a. Normal Achilles tendon, which has an even thickness and tapers towards its insertion into the heel bone. The tendon has a fascicular pattern with no swelling or calcifications.

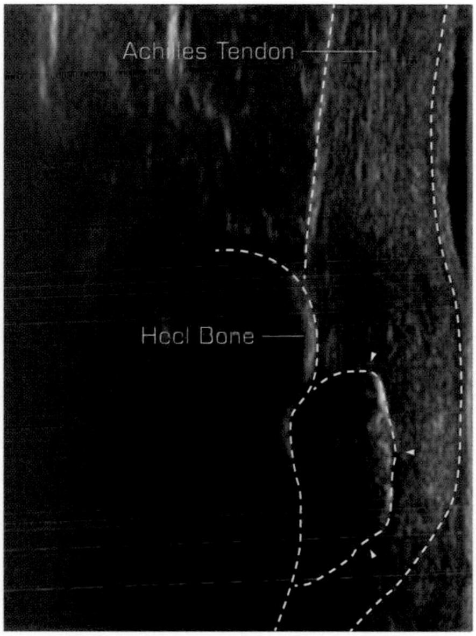

Figure 9.12b. Achilles enthesiopathy. A large calcification (arrows) accumulates at the insertion of the Achilles tendon into the heel bone.

The onset of pain is gradual, and is worse after training or in the early morning. Activities such as pushing off during running, stair climbing, and standing on tiptoe may be painful. Sudden and severe pain, often described as the sensation of being kicked on the back of the heel, suggests a rupture of the tendon.

Ice, anti-inflammatory medication, and physiotherapy are useful for pain relief. Shoe inserts such as heel lifts can help to reduce the load on the affected tendon. The Achilles tendon is slow to heal as it has a poor blood supply. To stimulate the repair processes, extra-corporeal shockwave therapy may be used, especially for Achilles enthesiopathy. Concurrently, the biomechanical causes need to be identified, via video gait analysis if necessary, and addressed before a full return to running.

● EXTRA CORPOREAL SHOCK WAVE THERAPY ●

Shock waves were first used to break kidney stones (extra corporeal shock wave lithotripsy) in 1980 and treat fracture non-unions in 1988. Since the 1990s, shock waves have been used to treat degenerative tendon-bone lesions (extra corporeal shock wave therapy, ESWT) as well. Such tendon-bone lesions include plantar fasciitis (see photo), Achilles enthesiopathy, patellar tendinosis, tennis and golfer's elbow, and calcific supraspinatus tendinopathy. Focal, ultrasound-guided shock waves have been shown to promote healing by stimulating the release of local growth factors. Its efficacy is reported at about 80 per cent. A typical course of treatment comprises two sessions; 2,000 pulses are fired over 10 minutes at each session. During treatment, the sensation is similar to that of being tapped deep inside by a small hammer.

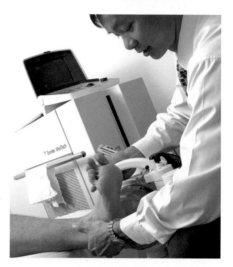

Medial Tibial Stress Syndrome

'Shin splint' is an old and non-specific term that can refer to a variety of shin conditions, so it is best to avoid its use. Medial tibial stress syndrome (MTSS) refers to diffuse pain along the inner border of the shinbone due to excessive traction of the deep calf muscles that are attached there. These muscles are activated during toe off and landing. MTSS tends to occur in those who step up their training load too quickly, and is therefore common several weeks after the start of the training cycle. The deep calf muscles help to hold up the medial longitudinal arch of the foot, and these muscles tend to be overloaded in those with flat feet, resulting in MTSS.

As the site of the pain is similar to that of a tibial stress fracture, it is important to differentiate MTSS from a stress fracture. This is because the management is totally different

— a runner diagnosed with MTSS can continue training, whereas a runner with a stress fracture should stop running completely until it heals.

MTSS can be seen as a problem of adaptation, where the attachments of the deep calf muscles have not adapted to the training load. By reducing the training load, by say 20 per cent and holding it there, it gives the attachment more time to consolidate. Once the pain eases, the training load can be increased. To accelerate the adaptation, soft tissue massage, stretching of the deep calf muscles, and correction of biomechanical factors are useful.

Stress Fractures

Bone reacts to repetitive loads by remodelling, a process whereby bone tissue is concurrently formed and removed to better tolerate the stress placed on it. If the bone is unable to remodel as quickly as the rate of increase in loading, a stress fracture could eventually develop. Mal-alignment (e.g. high medial arches), muscle weakness (muscles are important for shock absorption), certain running gaits, hard training surfaces,

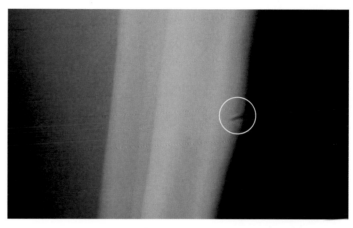

Figure 9.13. X-ray of a 32 year old female runner showing a chronic stress fracture at the anterior border of the tibia (circled).

running on sand (sand dampens the impact too much and robs the body of the rebound), and excessive body weight are other factors that makes one more prone to stress fractures. In runners, the tibia (shinbone), fibula, metatarsals, navicular (a bone in the mid foot), pelvic bone and thighbone are susceptible to stress fractures. Oestrogen, a female hormone that is deficient in women who stop menstruating due to rapid and excessive weight loss as well as postmenopausal women, is important for bone health. These women are therefore at risk of osteoporosis and stress fractures.

The onset of pain is gradual, and usually aggravated by weight bearing activities. There is a focal area of tenderness on the affected bone. In the early stages, stress fractures are not visible on X-rays (see figure 9.13). If a magnetic resonance imaging scan (MRI) is performed, it will show a well-localised area of bone swelling (marrow oedema). If the athlete ignores the symptoms and continues training, a frank fracture (an actual break in the bone) can develop.

A stress fracture spells an extended downtime for the runner, as bone healing is slow and cannot be rushed. It pays to detect a stress fracture early: if symptoms have been present for less than three weeks, then the average recovery time is 10 weeks; if the diagnosis is made more than three weeks after the onset of symptoms, then the recovery time averages 18 weeks. To facilitate recovery, all impact activities, especially running, should be stopped. A common mistake is to resume training once the pain ceases. This results in a recurrence, as the pain will stop before the healing is complete. Your doctor will advise you on how long you have to stop running, based on the severity of your stress fracture. Surgery may be necessary in bad and chronic cases. During the recuperation period, deep water running (see facing page) is a good way to maintain your fitness. Use this opportunity to cross train (e.g. cycling, swimming, rowing), do resistance training, and engage in core strengthening exercises.

Chronic Compartment Pressure Syndrome

The muscles of the leg are compartmentalised within fibrous fascial envelopes. When running, the muscles expand as they become engorged with blood. Usually, the envelope stretches with the expanding muscles, limiting the rise in pressure within the muscle compartment. But if the fascial envelope becomes rigid (eg. scarring or thickening from repetitive injury), the pressure rises excessively while running, causing incremental pain. Blood flow through compartment may be impeded and compression of the nerves within the compartment may cause numbness in the foot. The muscle may bulge out through deficient areas of the fascia.

The runner with chronic compartment pressure syndrome is pain-free at rest. When running, a dull ache and sensation of tightness begins after several minutes, and intensifies to an unbearable bursting sensation if the runner continues to run. The muscle becomes tense and rigid. When running stops, the pain takes 10 or more minutes to abate. To confirm the diagnosis, the high compartment pressures are documented with a catheter inserted into the compartment when the pain is at its peak.

To manage chronic compartment pressure syndrome, an attempt to 'loosen' the fascia is made via myofascial release techniques and stretching. If this fails, then a large window is surgically created in the fascia, allowing the muscle to expand through it during exercise.

DEEP WATER RUNNING

If you are recuperating from impact injuries (e.g. stress fracture), cross training, or wish to enhance recovery, deep water running is an excellent option. Of all the non-impact exercise modalities, it is the closest thing to actual running.

What you need is a pool deep enough such that your feet cannot touch the bottom of the pool. A floatation vest or belt helps keep your balance, but with practice, you can actually do without them. Here's how you do it:

Subject engaged in deep water running in Changi Sports Medicine Centre's hydropool.

- Get into the deep end of the pool such that the water level is up to your neck and your feet are off the floor.
- Start running in the water, while maintaining good running form. Run in the water as you would on land. Minimise unwanted movements such as flinging your arms. If you fail to maintain good running form, you may be reinforcing bad habits that may persist when you run on land.
- If you lean slightly forward, you will find yourself moving forward in the water.
- 'Run' along the breadth of the pool, back and forth. As in interval training, you can take a short break when you reach one end.
- The faster you move your limbs, the greater the water resistance, and the more intensive the workout.

Osteoarthritis

Osteoarthritis is simply wear and tear of the cartilage lining of the joint. Wear and tear is a normal part of the ageing process. However, excessive body weight, excessive use, and joint mal-alignment (as with bow legs, for example) accelerate the process (see figure 9.14). The cartilage may soften, fray, thin out or become ulcerated. At the same time, the joint fluid becomes less viscous and therefore less able to lubricate the joint. In runners, the weight bearing joints such as the knee, ankles, and hip can become osteoarthritic. The symptoms of osteoarthritis occur gradually, with diffused aching and swelling, especially after running. In advanced cases, the joint is visibly widened.

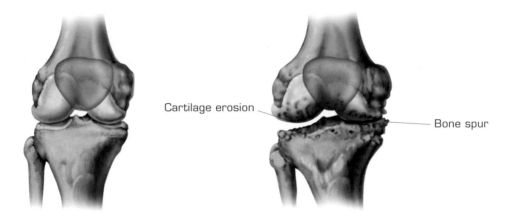

Cartilage erosion

Bone spur

Figure 9.14. A normal (left) and an osteoarthritic (right) knee

The cartilage lining the joint gets its nutrition mostly from the joint fluid. Joint movement has the effect of "pumping" the joint fluid into the cartilage matrix, thereby nourishing the cartilage cells. Hence, regular and moderate physical activities, such as running, are healthy and necessary for our joint health.

Is osteoarthritis inevitable in runners? Logic tells us that with excessive use, wear and tear will ultimately set in. But what is considered excessive? This is varies greatly between individuals. I have patients in their seventies who train regularly and participate in a few marathons a year. X-rays of their knees showed that they were no different from that of 35 year olds. Then there are younger patients who lead very sedentary lives, with X-rays showing marked osteoarthritis. It is impossible to define a threshold mileage beyond which osteoarthritis will occur, as every individual is different. Weight and joint alignment have a lot to do with it. Where your individual threshold mileage lies will have to be discovered by trial and error — for the majority of healthy individuals, the threshold is probably higher than they presume.

The treatment of osteoarthritis depends on its severity. It can range from cortisone injections and viscosupplementation (injection of "artificial lubricant" into the joint) to arthroscopic debridement (cleaning up the inside of the joint through keyhole surgery), microfracture (causing small fractures at the base of a cartilage ulcer to induce scar tissue to form over the ulcer), articular cartilage transplantation of the ulcerated area, and ultimately joint replacement. Your doctor will advice you of which option is best suited for you.

Glucosamine and chondroitin are popular over-the-counter medications used in the treatment of osteoarthritis. Studies have shown that glucosamine sulphate, in particular, is able to slow down or stop the further loss of cartilage, but it is very doubtful that it can help regenerate new cartilage. While its effect is not drastic (i.e. do not expect a miraculous improvement of any cartilage lesions), glucosamine sulphate has negligible side effects. If you wish to try it, follow the dosage that has been tried and tested in studies that have shown some efficacy, i.e. 1,500 milligrammes (mg) of glucosamine sulphate per day. It does not really matter how you divide the dose over the course of the day. Its effects will not be evident overnight, so you will need to take the medication continuously for about three months before deciding if it is helping you. If you find it useful, you will need to take it for life, as its action is lost when you stop taking it.

Chafing

Chafing develops when adjacent layers of skin run against each other, such as between the inner thighs or below the armpits. While not serious, chafing can be a major source of distraction during a run. This can be prevented by the generous application of Vaseline or other lubricants.

In men, repetitive friction between the nipples and clothing can cause painful abrasions or even bleeding. Use a lubricant or tape the nipples down to prevent this.

Blisters

Blisters erupting on the soles, toes, or back of the heel can be an unnecessary distraction during training or racing. They are usually the result of ill-fitting shoes or wet socks.

To prevent blisters, ensure that your shoes are neither too tight nor too loose. Never use a shoe for the first time during a race, even if you are using a familiar model. Pare down any existing calluses before a race. Apply lubricant on areas where you are prone to blisters. There are anti-blister plasters and anti-blister socks (e.g. a double-layered sock) that you can use.

If you do get a blister that is tense and painful, lance it with a clean needle to release the fluid and relieve the pressure. Keep the area clean and dry.

Subungal Haematomas

Repetitive impact against the front of the shoe (toe box) can lift the nail off the nail bed, with blood accumulating in the space in between. The nail turns black, and may or may not be painful. The cause is usually a shoe that is too loose, such that the foot slides forward and jams the nail against the front of the shoe; or it can be due to a tight-fitting shoe.

The subungal haematoma is painful when the build up of blood under the nail becomes tense. The pain is relieved the instant the blood is drained. To do this, straighten a paperclip and heat the tip till it is red-hot. Use the tip to burn a hole in the top of the nail. There is no need to forcefully pierce the nail — if the tip is hot enough, it will melt a tiny hole in the nail without force.

The black nail will take about six months to grow out and be replaced by a more normal looking nail. During this time, trim your nail regularly so that your shoe does not make the nail tear off.

Foot Corn and Callus

Corn and callus are both thickened areas of skin. A callus is a more spread out patch of thickened skin, whereas a corn is a thicker and more focal lesion. The formation of corns and calluses is the skin's natural attempt to protect against excessive pressure or friction. Initially this thickening of the skin is helpful, but over time the thickened mass results in increased pressure and discomfort, and a vicious cycle ensues.

The thickened skin of a corn appears as a conical mass, with the tip of the cone pointing down into the skin (see figure 9.15). The pressure from the point of the corn causes pain. It usually forms where there is

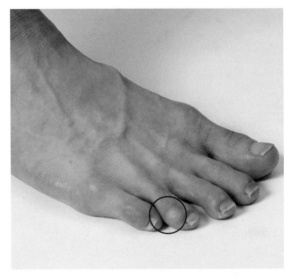

Figure 9.15. Corn on the 4th toe (circled)

a bony prominence, such as the top of toe joints, tips of the toe, and the ball of the foot. In dry areas, the corn is hard whereas in moist areas, such as between the toes, the corn can be soft. Corns are often mistaken for warts and vice versa, as they look fairly identical. A plantar wart is a skin growth caused by the human papilloma virus. It has a "cauliflower" appearance with a minute black spot that is noticeable under close scrutiny. Pain is elicited from a corn with direct pressure whereas with a wart, marked pain and discomfort is elicited by pinching of the lesion's border.

A callus is a diffused area of skin on the body that has become hard due to constant pressure or friction. In runners, calluses are commonly found at the border of the heel, the area around the big toe and the ball of the foot. When excessively thick, a painful blister can form under a callus.

To treat a corn or callus, the first step is to find the cause of the increased pressure or friction. A podiatrist may be able to help you identify and rectify the cause. Once the faulty foot mechanics are addressed, attempts can be made to treat the corn or callus itself. They can be trimmed with a blade or pumice stone, but do be careful not to break through the skin. Topical applications such as salicylic acid cannot differentiate the corn and callus from normal skin, causing the whole areas to be macerated. It would be safer to get your podiatrist to pare the corn or callus down for you.

PRE-HABILITATION

Since we know what the common running injuries are, why wait for the injuries to happen? There are exercises that we can do to prevent the common running injuries. For example, we know that the most common injury in the runner is patellofemoral (knee) pain syndrome, and that iliotibial band stretches are used to treat the condition. Instead of waiting for the onset of patellofemoral pain, we can add iliotibial band stretches to our usual stretching routine, thereby reducing the risk of patellofemoral pain syndrome.

Stretching, strengthening, and core training exercises should be done regularly, as they rectify many intrinsic factors that predispose a runner to injuries, thereby preventing common running injuries. The following stretching and strengthening exercises are some that you can incorporate into your workouts.

Stretching

Stretching relaxes muscles that may be tight as a result of cumulative tension after each run. Tightness of the hamstrings, calves, and hip muscles can lead to abnormal running biomechanics, thereby causing injuries and impeding performance. Stretching also forms one component of the runner's recovery strategy.

Perform the stretches shown on pages 150 – 155 daily, including your rest day. On your running and gym days, perform them before and after each run or gym session. Hold each stretch for 30 seconds and repeat three times.

GASTROCNEMIUS STRETCH

Place both palms flat on a wall. Put one leg in front of the other and lean forward. Your back knee should be extended.

Switch legs and repeat.

SOLEUS AND DEEP CALF STRETCH

Place both palms flat on a wall. Put one leg in front of the other and lean toward the wall. Bend both your knees as though you are about to sit down.

Switch legs and repeat.

QUADRICEPS STRETCH

Stand upright and hold onto your foot or ankle. Gently pull your foot or ankle toward your buttocks.

Switch sides and repeat.

ITB STRETCH

Stand upright with your hands on your hips. Cross your left leg over your right and lean towards your left.

Switch legs and repeat.

HAMSTRING STRETCH (SITTING OPTION)

Sit on the ground and stretch your right leg out. Keeping your knee as straight as you can, lean forward slowly and towards your toes.

Switch legs and repeat.

HAMSTRING STRETCH (STANDING OPTION)

Place your right leg in front of the left. Your right knee should be straight. Place your hands just above your knee. Bend your left knee as though you are about to sit down.

Switch legs and repeat.

ADDUCTOR STRETCH

Sit on the ground and place your feet sole-to-sole,
holding onto your ankles. Use your elbows to
gently push down on your knees and lean forward
slowly. Pull your heels toward your body if you are
unable to feel the stretch.

ADDUCTOR STRETCH OPTION

Assume a squatting position and fully extend your
right leg out toward the side.

Switch sides and repeat.

GLUTEAL STRETCH

Sit on the ground with legs outstretched.Cross
your right leg over left (knee should be bent).
Use your left arm to push your right knee further
toward the left.

Switch sides and repeat.

PSOAS STRETCH

Adopt a forward lunge position, with your left leg in front. Drop your right knee. Place your hands over your left knee and push your pelvis forward gently.

Switch sides and repeat.

LOWER BACK STRETCH

Kneel on the ground. Lower yourself until your face is nearly touching the ground. Extend your arms in front of you and round your back.

COBRA/MACKENZIE STRETCH

Lie face down on the ground. Use your arms to slowly push your upper body up.

PIRIFORMIS STRETCH

Lie flat on the ground. Bend your left knee and cross your right leg over it. Using your arms, pull your left knee towards your chest while keeping your right knee away.

Switch legs and repeat.

PIRIFORMIS STRETCH OPTION

Sit on a chair. Bring up your right leg, your ankle resting just a little above the left knee. Keeping your back straight, lean your body forward gently while pushing your right knee down with your elbow.

Switch legs and repeat.

TRUNK ROTATION

Lying flat on the ground, bend your right knee and cross it over to your left. Extend your right arm and reach out toward the right.

Switch sides and repeat.

VASTUS LATERALIS STRETCH

Lie on your left side, with your head on your left arm. Use your right hand to pull your right foot or ankle towards your buttock. Use your left foot to press your knee down towards the floor.

Switch sides and repeat.

Strengthening Exercises

High impact activities such as running place a lot of stress on our musculoskeletal system. There is nothing to fear if our bodies have adapted to the stress. Some muscles act eccentrically during running, i.e. the muscle actively contracts while it is stretching out. An example is the hamstring, which lengthens as the lower limb swings forward; but contracts at the same time to decelerate the forward swing. The opposing action (eccentric action) places great stress on the muscle, often leading to tears. To be able to tolerate eccentric action, the muscles need to be strong and well-conditioned.

Apart from being more resistant to tears, strong muscles serve as excellent shock absorbers. By absorbing shock, the muscles reduce the jarring and tensile forces within the tendons, their insertions into the bone, and the bones and joints, thereby reducing the risk of tendinopathies, enthesiopathies, stress fractures, and joint injuries.

Apart from preventing injuries, strength training also confers performance advantages:

- The ability to ramp up the power in scenarios such as sprint finishes, hill climbs, and overtaking

- Improved running economy

- Delayed fatigue. In a strong muscle, fewer motor units (a motor unit comprises a nerve and the muscle fibre it supplies) need to be activated to produce a given force, thus delaying fatigue

- Optimal utilization of the stretch-shortening cycle (SSC) during ground contact. The SSC stores the elastic recoil from the landing of the foot to recycle the energy into the next step.

The exercises that follow represent a basic collection of strengthening exercises for the runner. They should be performed once or twice a week, on your non-running day. At each session, perform three sets of 12 repetitions (progressively build up towards this). The load used (if any) should be heavy enough for you to just complete 12 repetitions with good form. Technique is important, not only to get the intended effect, but also to prevent injuries — enlist a qualified trainer to show you how to perform the exercises correctly if you are not experienced. The dead lift is especially injurious — if you are new at weight training, do the hamstring curl instead. Upper body exercises are not shown in the chart, but it would be good to perform them (e.g. push ups, pull ups, one-arm rowing) for a more balanced muscular development. While strengthening of the lower body is essential to running, the body's core must not be neglected. You can refer to pages 162 – 172 for some core exercises you can try.

SINGLE-LEG CALF RAISES WITH DUMBBELL

Hold onto a support to stabilise yourself and stand on the edge of a stepboard or step. Bend your left leg 90° behind you and stand on the ball of your right foot, holding the dumbbell in your right hand. Push yourself up using your right foot to a tip-toe position.

LUNGES WITH DUMBBELLS

Hold one dumbbell in each hand. Lunge forward, keeping your back straight.

DEAD LIFT *

Hold the barbell just below knee level in front of you. Keep your back straight. Then straighten your knees and back until you are in a standing position.

HAMSTRING CURL *

Hold onto a support to stabilise yourself. Loop an exercise band around your foot and tie its ends securely to the base of the support. Bring your foot towards your buttock.

HIP FLEXION

Stand in front of a support and loop an exercise band around your ankle and tie its ends securely to the base of the support. Place your hands on your hips and lift your knee to about 90°.

* Do either the dead lift or the hamstring curl — if you are new to resistance training, avoid doing the dead lift.

Forty-eight year old Malaysian Ng Seow Kong is a marathoner and ultramarathoner who has run 50 marathons/ultramarathons (as of June 09), including adventure marathons like the Everest Tenzing Hillary Marathon (world's highest marathon at an altitude of more than 5,300 m), North Pole, Antarctica, Sahara Desert 100 km (see photo), North Face 100 km, Comrade Marathons (87 km & 89 km), Great Wall Marathon, and more. He is the first Asian (and 28th in the world) able-bodied person to have completed the Grand Slam marathons (comprising marathons in the seven continents of Asia, Europe, Oceania, Africa, North America, South America and Antarctica, plus the North Pole). How does the man endure so much punishment? Here are his training tips:

"When training as a distance runner, there are many aspects of training to look at. To me, the three most important ones are: Firstly the mental discipline to 'push' and 'pull' appropriately; Secondly, cross training, including strength training, and; Thirdly, flexibility training.

"For the same weekly mileage covered, one should avoid pushing for a fast time for every single run. Instead, learn to force yourself to slow down so as to allow your body to recover for the hard and fast runs in later days. Running should not be the only sport that a runner gets involved in — time must be set aside to engage in other sporting activities such as working out in the gym. Sufficient time must also be allowed (especially for older runners) for flexibility exercises immediately before or after each run and also the non-running days. I do flexibility exercises for about an hour almost every single night. I also attend yoga classes once a week (or more often if I can) to ensure my muscles are as relaxed as possible.

"Each of these three aspects will, on its own, improve your speed, increase running longevity and lessen injuries. When taken together, you'll discover a new level of the joy of running!"

Core Training for the Runner
The Importance of Core Training.

As a runner, you cannot afford to leave core training out of your regular training program. Training your core muscles not only improves your running economy, it also enables you to tolerate high training mileages without sustaining injuries. The aim of training your core is ultimately to improve your running form and enable you to propel your body forwards by leading with your core muscles and not with your leg or arm muscles.

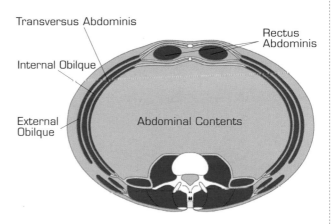

Figure 9.16. Transverse section of the trunk, showing the major core muscles.

This might seem like a foreign idea; think of your core as the centre of all your running movements and initiate your running movements from the core, so brace your core, rotate the hips and lift your knee, as opposed to starting your movement with your foot and then your knee and hips following. As much as there is a lot of talk about core training, many people do not train their core correctly. The first thing you need to do is to get acquainted with your core muscles.

Where Are My Core Muscles? Many may think that core muscle training involves doing sit-ups and abdominal crunches. These exercises preferentially train one particular abdominal muscle, the rectus abdominis or the 'six-pack.' Anatomically this muscle attaches the ribcage above to the pelvis below from the front. Being the furthest from the spine, the rectus abdominis has the least ability in providing protective stability to the spine.

You do not need an impressive six-pack to be a good runner — what you do need are strong deep core stabilizers. These are the deep abdominal muscles comprising, from deep to superficial, the transversus abdominis (TA), internal obliques (IO) and external obliques (EO). The most important of the three is the TA (see figure 9.16). The TA wraps around the entire torso, acting like a natural corset that provides support and keeps the lumbar spine stable. In addition to assisting the TA, the IO and EO rotate the trunk. The EO on one side contracts simultaneously with the IO on the opposite side to bring about trunk rotation.

Other supporting muscles help to form the core, including:

- The diaphragm, which forms the roof of the torso
- The pelvic floor muscles which forms the floor of the torso
- The multifidus muscles, which are found on either side of the spinal column
- The psoas major muscle which forms part of the posterior abdominal wall

Core Training Principles. The principles underlining core training include:

- **Centering.** Finding the centre is the beginning, as doing so will ensure that with all exercises and ultimately with running, the effort comes mainly from the centre (core) and not from the limbs.

  To do the centering exercise, we first need to find our TA, which is to be our centre or our core. You may begin practicing this lying down on an exercise mat with feet flat on the mat. Place your index and middle fingers on your abdomen, approximately an inch inwards and downwards from the bony prominence at the front of your pelvis (see figure 9.17). Now, imagine that there is a taut string linking both bony prominences, embedded within your abdomen. Gently, think of shortening the string and pulling the two bony prominences together. Feel your abdomen tighten under your fingers. Maintain this tension while taking regular breaths. Alternatively, you can try activating your TA by thinking of a string pulling your belly button down towards your spine. You may also try recruiting your pelvic floor muscles by tightening the muscles that stops the flow of urine.

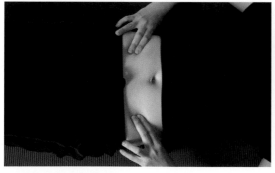 

Figure 9.17. Finding your centre.

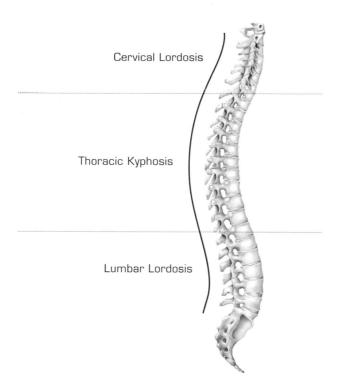

Cervical Lordosis

Thoracic Kyphosis

Lumbar Lordosis

Figure 9.18. Lateral view of spinal column showing a neutral spine, with normal thoracic kyphosis and lumbar lordosis.

- **Optimal Spinal Alignment.** Many core exercises require your spinal alignment to be in the neutral position, where there is least strain and tension on any particular segment of the spine. In this neutral position, the natural spinal curvatures are preserved and the ribcage is positioned optimally over the pelvic girdle (see figure 9.18). Poor spinal alignment is a common fault, and awareness of this is the beginning for change.

  To practice getting into the neutral spinal posture, stand with your back flat against a wall with knees slightly bent, placing one hand on your breastbone and another on your pubic bone. Make minor adjustments till both hands fall on a straight vertical line. The space between your lower back and the wall should be minimal.

  Depending on the difficulty of the exercise, some intermediate and advanced exercises require that you lose the neutral spine and flatten your lower back such that there is no space between the lower back and supporting surface. This is done to protect your back. Failing to flatten the back slightly when performing such exercises increases the strain on the lumbar spine.

- **Respiration.** The third element for core training is respiration or breathing. The diaphragm forms the roof of the torso and plays a role in core training and breathing. An inefficient breathing pattern results in the excessive use of neck and abdominal muscles, thus compromising running economy and running performance.

  A common complaint when performing the centering exercise is breathlessness. This happens when you pull and tighten your abdomen excessively, making it hard for the diaphragm to move down as you inhale. To compensate, your accessory breathing muscles such as those in the neck have to be activated to lift your rib cage (thoracic, or chest, breathing) further, resulting in a laboured breathing pattern.

  The efficient breathing pattern to adopt while still activating your core muscles is to allow your belly to distend slightly during inhalation (abdominal breathing) so that only a comfortable level of thoracic breathing is required. This limited abdominal breathing pattern allows the diaphragm to assist in inhalation while maintaining TA tension. This ideal breathing pattern should be maintained while running.

- **Ease.** The final principle is that the exercises should be performed with as much ease as possible, while maintaining good form. Tensing the TA while breathing with the diaphragm may not feel natural initially, but it will come with practice. Optimal spinal alignment facilitates this breathing pattern.

  The ideal sensation when performing the above breathing and posture is heaviness and tensioning of the lower abdominal area and nowhere else. There should be a subtle flattening of the lower abdomen, no tension in the low back, and minimal or no tension in arms and legs.

Core Training Exercises. First practice the centering, neutral spine, and breathing exercises as described above. Next, go through the selection of core training exercises (including elements of Pilates) that follows, starting at the beginner's level. Progress to the intermediate, then advanced exercises over several weeks. Note that Exercise 1 is performed with a neutral spine position, while the rest are performed with a flattened lower back. Technique is key, and if you have difficulty, engage a qualified instructor to supervise you.

BEGINNER: FEMUR ARCS (WITH ASSISTANCE USING FITBALL)

- Lie with heels of both feet resting on fitball and both thighs vertical. Observe centering and breathing.

- Inhale to prepare. Exhale and extend one leg by pushing fitball away. Keep your centre heavy and grounded towards the mat while imagining that the legs are light as feather resting on a bubble.

- Inhale and bring leg back to starting position. Repeat with other leg. Keep alternating. Perform for 1 minute. Repeat a maximum of 3 minutes.

- Do not lower the leg too far down if you feel that you have lost your centre or your back has lifted off the mat.

INTERMEDIATE: FEMUR ARCS

- Lie with both feet up in the air, both thighs vertical, and knees flexed to 90°. Observe centering and breathing.

- Keep a neutral spine position. Inhale to prepare. Exhale and lower one leg to the floor, lightly tapping your toes on the mat.

- Inhale and bring leg back to starting position. Repeat with other leg. Keep alternating. Imagine that there are puppet strings pulling your knees up and lowering them down slowly. Perform slowly with control for 1 minute. Repeat maximum of 3 minutes.

- Do not lower the foot too far down if you feel that you have lost your centre or your back has lifted off the mat.

ADVANCED: FEMUR ARCS WITH HEAD AND CHEST LIFTED

- Same as intermediate exercise but performed with head and chest lifted.

CORE TRAINING EXERCISE 2: BRIDGING SERIES

BEGINNER: BRIDGING

- Lie face up with feet flat on the floor. Maintain neutral spine and observe breathing and centering. Inhale to prepare. Keeping the upper body and arms relaxed, slowly roll the spine up, from tailbone upwards. Roll the pelvis backwards, use your centre to lift from the tailbone, peeling your spine segment by segment off the mat.

- Once at the top, inhale to prepare.

- Exhale and begin segmentally rolling back down, ensuring that the movement is as slow and controlled as possible and with as much ease as possible, until the tailbone rests back on the floor to resume the neutral position. Perform for 1 minute. Repeat for maximum of 3 minutes.

INTERMEDIATE: BRIDGING WITH FEMUR ARCS

- Lie face up with feet flat on the floor. Maintain neutral spine and observe breathing and centering. Inhale to prepare. Keeping the upper body and arms relaxed, slowly roll the spine up, from tailbone upwards. Roll the pelvis backwards, use your centre to lift from the tailbone, peeling your spine segment by segment off the mat.

- Once at the top, inhale as you lift one foot off the floor while keeping the rest of the body stable.

- Exhale and lower leg down. Repeat with other leg. Keep alternating slowly.

- After completing 1 minute of this, end with both feet on the ground. Inhale at the top to prepare.

- Exhale and begin segmentally rolling back down, ensuring that the movement is as slow and controlled as possible and with as much ease as possible, until the tailbone rests back on the floor to resume the neutral position.

- Repeat for maximum of 3 minutes.

ADVANCED: BRIDGING WITH FEMUR ARCS, FEET ON FOAM ROLLER

- Bridging as an exercise can be further progressed by placing the feet on a foam roller. The unstable foam roller raise the degree of difficulty, as you will need to engage your core muscles more in order to maintain stability. Bear in mind that performing the exercise on a foam roller may be too difficult for you if you find yourself holding your breath, if you feel back ache and/or feel that you are using your gluteal (buttock) and hamstring muscles more than your core muscles during the exercise.

BEGINNER: ROLL DOWN (WITH ARM SUPPORT)

- Sit fairly upright with hands holding the side of thighs gently. Inhale to prepare.
- Exhale and slowly roll the spine down, pulling the belly button down to spine, and go as far as you can while keeping both feet on the mat.
- At the bottom, maintain the spine curved into a letter "C". Inhale to prepare. Return to upright position as you exhale.
- Perform for 1 minute. Repeat over 3 minutes.

INTERMEDIATE: ROLL UP/DOWN

- Lie face up with leg extended and arms stretched above head. Observe centering and inhale to prepare.
- While engaging your core, slowly peel your spine off the mat segmentally, from top down, until you are sitting upright. Exhale on your way up.
- Inhale to prepare. Exhale to slowly lower the back segmentally, from bottom to top.
- Perform for 1 minute. Repeat over 3 minutes.

ADVANCED: ROLL DOWN (WITH HANDS BEHIND HEAD)

- As previous exercise but with the hands clasped behind the head.

CORE TRAINING EXERCISE 4:   HUNDREDS SERIES

BEGINNER: WITH KNEES AT 90°

- Adopt same position as the exercises for "femur arcs".
- Raise chest and shoulders off mat using your core as you exhale.
- With palms facing the ceiling, inhale in 5 counts while pressing your palms upwards for 5 counts.
- With palms facing the mat, exhale in 5 counts while pressing your palms in a pumping action downwards for 5 counts.
- Repeat 5 counts with inhalation and 5 counts for exhalation. You will the complete 100 counts in a total of 10 breaths.

INTERMEDIATE: WITH KNEES STRAIGHT AND HIPS AT 45°

• As previous exercise but with leg straight and raised.

ADVANCED: STRAIGHT LEGS, JUST OFF THE GROUND

• As above but with the legs as low as you can manage without lifting the lower back off the mat.

CORE TRAINING EXERCISE 5: SIDE PLANK SERIES

BEGINNER: SIDE PLANK WITH KNEES AT 90°

- Lie on your side with your knees bent to 90°. Observe centering. Inhale to prepare.
- Exhale as you lift the side of your trunk off the floor till your spine is in neutral position.
- Hold for 10 seconds while maintaining regular breathing.
- Return to the original position as you exhale.
- Perform for 1 minute. Repeat a maximum of 3 minutes.
- Do the same for the other side.

INTERMEDIATE: SIDE PLANK WITH UPPER KNEE STRAIGHT

- Progress by extending the top leg.

ADVANCED: SIDE PLANK WITH BOTH KNEES STRAIGHT

- Progress by extending both legs.

- You can make it even more difficult by abducting the top leg and holding for 10 seconds.

CORE TRAINING EXERCISE 6: PRONE PLANK WITH HIP FLEXION

- Adopt quadruped position, with both palms and knees on the floor. The arms and thighs should be vertical.

- To move into the prone plank position, straighten one knee at a time and end with both knees straight and your weight on the ball of your feet. Maintain neutral spine during plank pose.

- Engage the core muscles. Inhale and pull one knee towards the chest while keeping pelvis stable.
- Exhale and return leg to original position. Repeat with the other leg.
- Perform the exercise for 1 minute. Repeat for a total of 3 minutes.

CORE TRAINING EXERCISE 7: TRUNK AND PELVIS ROTATION

BEGINNER: TRUNK ROTATION WITH FITBALL

- Lie face up. Place the legs on a fitball.
- Assume position with the thighs vertical and arms resting slightly away from torso on the floor.
- Inhale and slowly allow the fitball to roll to right side, controlling the motion. Keep your left shoulder firmly resting on the mat.
- Exhale and bring the fitball back to the original position. Draw together a point from the front of your right pelvis to the front of the left chest. By doing this, you are using your left EO and right IO to bring the fitball back to original position.
- Repeat to the left.
- Perform the exercise for 1 minute. Repeat for a total of 3 minutes.

INTERMEDIATE: TRUNK ROTATION WITHOUT FITBALL

- Perform the same exercise without the help of a fitball.

ADVANCED: TRUNK ROTATION WITH KNEES STRAIGHT

- Bring arms closer to torso, and rotate further such that legs reach closer to mat. To make it even more challenging, extend your knees while keeping the hips flexed to 90°.

RECOVERY

A competitive runner must perform a fine balancing act between training and recovery. On the one hand, the runner needs a high training load to induce adaptations that will make him perform better, on the other hand, he needs to recover quickly enough to tolerate the high training load (see figure 9.19). The faster his recovery, the higher the training load he can tolerate without injury. If he is slow to recover, injury and overtraining syndrome results.

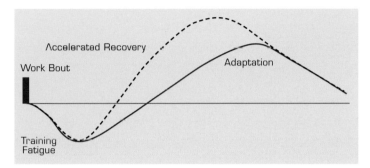

Figure 9.19. Immediately after a workout, performance drops over the course of one to two days due to fatigue (solid line). Soon, we recover beyond our pre-exercise level of fitness (supercompensation) and adapt to the exercise bout. However, this supercompensation phase does not last forever — our fitness level falls back to the baseline level about four days after the bout of exercise. With good recovery strategies, recovery is accelerated (dotted line).

A recovery strategy comprises sports massage, stretching, good wholesome nutrition, active rest (e.g. doing light cross training such as swimming and cycling on your non-running days), and a periodized training programme that incorporates taper and transition phases. All, except sports massage, have been covered earlier.

Sports Massage

What is Sports Massage? Many are confused as to what sports massage entails, and what sets it apart from other forms of massage. Sports massage is an anatomically based form of massage that aims to enhance recovery, prevent injuries, and manage injuries. Apart from sports massage and Swedish massage, practically all other forms of massage have an underlying mystic that is hard to define, such as unblocking 'energy' lines, releasing 'wind,' restoring 'balance,' detoxifying, restoring '*qi*.' Sports massage, on the other hand, is simply based on human anatomy and physiology.

Techniques. Various sports massage techniques are used to achieve different objectives. For example, effleurage (light, superficial, and broad strokes) warms and relaxes the muscles; kneading goes deeper and reduces muscle tone and promotes circulation; stroking promotes circulation and lymphatic drainage; deep friction releases knotted muscles and scar tissue; and tapotement (tapping) invigorates the athlete (usually done just before an event).

Deleterious Effects of Prolonged Training. With prolonged training, our muscles tend to get stiff. Localised areas of spasm, called trigger points or knots, accumulate in the muscles and these are felt as painful lumps during massage. The knotted areas are less contractile and therefore less able to perform their function, leaving the runner with a smaller area of 'useable' muscle. As the unaffected muscle has to perform the work of the whole muscle, they too get fatigued and knotted up. Soon, the runner ends up with a stiff, tight, and easily fatigued muscle. The trigger points tend to accumulate in predictable areas, such as the gluteus medius (hip abductor), vastus lateralis, and hamstrings as these are muscles that are subjected to high loads during running. In those with faulty running gaits, the resulting overloaded muscles tend to get knotted up as well. An example is the piriformis muscle, which is overloaded and goes into spasm in those whose lower limb deviates from the saggital plane (e.g. their feet swing outwards) during the forward swing. Another example is the deep posterior compartment (the muscles just behind the shinbone), which tightens and gets knotted up in flat-footed runners as the collapsed medial arch pulls excessively on those muscles.

With prolonged training, micro tears in the muscles result in scarring and fibrous tissue. Waste products such as lactic acid may also accumulate in the muscles. The over trained, nervous, or stressed runner can have an excitable nervous system, resulting in tense muscles throughout the body.

Benefits and Effects of Sports Massage. Runners therefore benefit from sports massage in several ways:

- Improved circulation of blood and lymphatic fluid through the muscles, which may promote repair and healing
- Improved flexibility
- Relief of delayed onset muscle soreness (DOMS)
- Accelerated recovery between training sessions
- Breaking down of adhesions and fibrous tissues
- Relaxation and prevention of trigger points

- Rehabilitation, e.g. release of the outer quadriceps to improve patellar tracking
- Relaxation of the nervous system

Frequency of Sports Massage. How much sports massage a runner needs depends mostly on his or her training load and injury status. The frequency may range from two massage sessions a week as the runner peaks for a race, to once a month during the off-season. For the most part of the training cycle, weekly or fortnightly sports massage would usually suffice for most runners.

If unable to afford the time, you can massage yourself using a mechanized handheld massager, hand roller, foam roller, tennis ball, or trigger ball.

Timing. The last deep sports massage is conducted preferably three to four days preceding an event. Doing it too close to the race day, such as the day before, may be detrimental to performance due to the excessively low muscle tone. Do stick to a sports massage therapist that you are familiar with as you should not try anything new before a major race. Just before the race (e.g. one to two hours), some may go for a light invigorating massage, much like what a boxer has just before his bout.

Post-event sports massage is done two to three days after a race. It is primarily aimed at enhancing recovery. The techniques employed are geared toward reducing the muscle spasms and lactic acid build-up.

HEAT INJURIES

Runners in the tropics often have to contend with a hot and humid environment during a marathon. When we run, a large proportion of the energy we expend is converted into heat rather than being used in the work of running. This raises heat production 10 – 20 times higher than at rest and increases the internal temperature (core temperature). An excessive rise in core temperature interferes with the function of muscles (leading to poorer performance) and also increases fatigue. High core temperatures also lead to damage to the cells and cause organ injury.

Heat injuries comprise heat cramps, heat exhaustion, and heat stroke. Tolerance for a rise in body temperature amongst athletes varies but heat exhaustion is often seen when the core temperature reaches 39 – 40°C. The risk of heat stroke rises when the core temperature exceeds 40°C.

The body removes the extra heat by diverting the blood flow to the skin where it may be lost to the environment through:

- Radiation: Heat is converted to infra-red waves and emitted off
- Conduction: Heat is transferred to the surrounding air
- Convection: Heat is carried by the circulating air as it passes over the skin
- Evaporation: Heat energy is removed as water in sweat is converted from its liquid state to the vapour state

Evaporative heat loss is the most significant; it accounts for 80 per cent of the heat removed from the body. Humid conditions impede evaporation, putting the runner at risk of heat injuries. Perspiring alone, without evaporation (e.g. sweating dripping off), results in fluid loss without significant heat removal. Bear in mind that a high relative humidity can also exist in a cool environment. For example, the relative humidity in Singapore is the lowest at noon time (approximately 60 per cent) and highest at about one o'clock in the morning (approximately 90 per cent). The cool environment should not lead to a false sense of security about the effects of heat stress. Running attires made of sweat wicking materials are not likely to be as effective in promoting heat removal when running in humid conditions because heat removal is limited by the lower rate of sweat evaporation and not by the wicking of the sweat.

The body faces the conflicting demands of having to supply blood to the skin to lose heat and at the same time supply blood to the muscles during exercise. The average person has about five litres of blood. When perspiration takes place, this volume of blood is reduced (volume contraction) because water is removed from our circulation, and this compounds the above problem. Hence it is important to maintain the volume of blood as much as possible through replenishing what water we have lost through sweating with drinking. This is especially so as the body adapts to exercising in a hot environment by sweating even more profusely, leading to dehydration, fatigue, and poor running performance. Running performance is compromised when you lose as little as 2 per cent of your body weight in water. Lose between 3 to 5 per cent, and your body's ability to remove excess heat becomes compromised. Profuse sweating also results in salt losses that put you at risk of heat cramps.

Heat cramps

Exertional heat cramps refer to the severe, sustained, and spreading cramping of the limbs and abdomen, that may accompany prolonged exercise in a hot environment. A milder form of exercise-associated muscle cramp can be seen in runners purely as a result of fatigue while exertional heat cramps are more associated with sodium depletion. It is fairly common and affects about one to two in every 1,000 racers. This tends to occur during prolonged races or races that run over consecutive days when there is water and salt loss through profuse perspiration. Runners who are unacclimatised to the heat conserve less salt, and end up losing more salt in their sweat than acclimatised runners, making them more prone to heat cramps. Acclimatised runners tend to have higher sweat rates and are thus also at risk of heat cramps.

To treat heat cramps, firmly stretch the cramped muscles. Drink adequate fluids to replace what you lost during the run and replace the salt (⅛ to ¼ of table salt or one to two salt tablets dissolved in half a litre of sports drink). Alternatively, increase the salt intake in your diet for the rest of the day to replace the salt lost in the long run.

To prevent heat cramps, supplement your diet with 5 – 10 g of salt a day before the run. During the run, replace water and salt losses. Use sports drink rather than plain water for replacement, or add salt to your replenishment fluids. Swallowing salt tablets during a run might lead to abdominal discomfort, so it would be better when added to fluids.

Heat Exhaustion

This refers to the inability to continue exercise when you are exerting in a hot environment. The runner is often tired and profusely perspiring and "collapses" onto the ground with fatigue but is still lucid. He or she may also experience nausea and vomiting, dizziness, chills, headache and weakness. The core body temperature is usually less than 40°C. A widespread dilation of the peripheral blood vessels triggers the phenomenon. The increased vascular space, together with the reduced circulating blood volume that is brought about by dehydration, causes the blood pressure to drop, leading to the exhaustion. It is now believed that the relaxation of the blood vessel is triggered by signals from the brain, and might be nature's safety mechanism to stop the runner from going on and averting a heat stroke. Risk factors for heat exhaustion include exercising in a hot and humid environment, dehydration, and a high body mass index.

Runners with exertional heat exhaustion need prompt treatment. Move the runner to a cool, shaded environment. Get the runner to lie on his/her back and elevate his/her feet to improve blood flow back to the heart. If available, cool the runner by applying ice bags to the armpit, neck and groin regions. If he or she is able to drink, encourage the runner to take rehydration fluids and seek medical attention. The runner needs to be monitored for a period of time to ensure that the hydration is adequate and that blood pressure improves. Conversely, if his/her condition deteriorates, intravenous replacement of fluids may be necessary. Even if the runner recovers from his/her symptoms with treatment, he or she has to continue taking in fluids till fully hydrated (the urine turns to a light straw colour). Rest for a day or two before resuming training and start off with light training in the cooler part of the day.

Heat Stroke

This is the most severe in the spectrum of heat injuries. The runner with heat stroke usually has an elevated core temperature more than 40°C, which can lead to the impairment of brain function and other organs.

Heat stroke tends to occur with high intensity exercise (thus increasing heat generation) in hot and humid environment where it is difficult to remove excess heat when the exercise is prolonged for more than an hour. It tends to occur in the unfit, dehydrated runner, but neither good physical fitness nor adequate water intake means that one will not suffer from heat stroke. Other contributing factors include a sudden increase in training volume, inadequate sleep, inadequate nutrition and hydration, recent viral illnesses, vomiting and diarrhoea (leading to dehydration), sunburn, unaccustomed exercise in hot and humid surroundings, certain medications, past history of heat injuries, and obesity.

The symptoms of heat stroke are non-specific and vary between each individual. They include those attributable to altered brain function (irritability, personality changes, headache, disorientation, confusion, and seizure), fatigue, loss of co-ordination, vomiting, diarrhoea, and collapse.

The afflicted runner would need urgent medical attention as early diagnosis and prompt treatment can avert death and organ failure. The runner should adhere strictly to his/her doctor's advice regarding return to sport.

Heat Acclimatisation

An improvement in thermoregulation will result in a lower body temperature when running under the same environmental conditions. Such an adaptation can prolong the duration of the run before reaching a body temperature that is too high to be tolerated. Thermoregulation can be improved and the risk of heat injuries reduced, through a process known as heat acclimatization. Heat acclimatization conditions the runner to run under hotter environmental conditions by running in the heat (condition of race) daily for 10 – 14 days. Physiological adaptations in heat acclimatization can be observed after three to four days. No further adaptations are observed after 14 days. The intensity and duration of the run, and the environmental condition during heat acclimatisation should reflect the race condition as much as possible. Running intensity and duration should be moderate (50 – 60 per cent of race performance) in the initial three to five days and increased gradually (close to race performance) over the 14 days of heat acclimatisation. Runners should aim to achieve about one to two hours of continuous run daily towards the 14th day of heat acclimatisation. Runners racing in hotter conditions overseas should undergo a period of heat acclimatisation locally first, and allow another week of heat acclimatization in the location of the race overseas.

EXERCISE ASSOCIATED HYPONATRAEMIA

Hyponatraemia refers to low sodium concentration in the serum. The concentration of sodium in the body should be kept within a tight range as it influences cellular function as well as the water content in the cells. Importantly, hyponatraemia causes the brain to swell.

Exercise associated hyponatraemia can occur in healthy people who have perspired profusely during exercise (i.e. losing water and salt) and then overzealously replaced the water loss without replacing the salt loss. It is often mistaken for heat exhaustion or heat stroke. Hyponatraemia occurs in prolonged events usually of more than three hours. Slower runners are at higher risk as they have sufficient time to drink enough water to exceed their sweat loss.

Hyponatraemia may manifest as nausea, vomiting, fatigue, dizziness, headache, bloatedness, cramps, shortness of breath, and collapse. These signs may occur at the end of the run or three to six hours after the run. The symptoms are non-specific and similar to heat stroke. As a hyponatraemic runner is not dehydrated, he does not have a loss in bodyweight and his core temperature is normal. Measuring the serum sodium concentration confirms the diagnosis.

All suspected cases require medical attention. Treatment for mild cases involves replacement of salt loss orally; more severe cases require intravenous replacement.

SUDDEN DEATH

Sudden Death in Sports is Rare

Sudden death refers to unexpected death from non-traumatic causes. For example, you may have seen media reports of apparently healthy runners collapsing during distance running events. Unexpected cases such as those tend to be sensationalised, giving people the impression that they are common. However, from the data available, it is quite clear that sudden death in sports is relatively uncommon in Singapore, as is the case in other parts of the world. The Department of Forensic Medicine, Health Sciences Authority (Singapore), reported a total of 15 deaths that occurred during sports in 2005 and 2006. During the same period, there were a total of 32,608 deaths (all causes). Thus, the 15 sports-related deaths during those two years accounted for only 0.046 per cent of deaths in Singapore, or one in 2,174 deaths. In 2005, there were nine sports-related deaths; the annual incidence was only 1 in 239,000 people who exercised at least once a week. In comparison, the annual incidence of sudden death of in runners the United States more than 35 years old is 1 in every 15,000 to 18,000 previously 'healthy' persons.

Causes of Sudden Death

There are a variety of causes of sudden death and their prevalence varies with age group. In all age groups, acute illness and external factors such as heat stroke and viral infection involving the heart (myocarditis) can cause sudden death in otherwise fit individuals with no previous history of heart disease. Doping (use of performance-enhancing drugs) with substances such as amphetamines and erythropoietin can potentially cause sudden death as well.

The incidence of sudden death in young athletes is around 1 in 133,000 males and 1 in 769,000 females. Half of these deaths were due to hypertrophic cardiomyopathy (enlargement of the heart muscle in excess of what would be expected as a response to training), with others due to coronary artery anomalies, myocarditis, and other less common causes. In the older age group (above 35 years), and in contrast to the young athletes, coronary artery disease resulting in acute myocardial infarction (heart attack) is the most common cause.

Does Exercise Increase the Risk of Acute Cardiovascular Events?

Acute cardiovascular events refer to sudden adverse events occurring in the heart, such as a sudden blockage of the arteries, sudden occurrence of irregular heart rhythm or the sudden rupture of the main blood vessel leaving the heart or the heart's valves. The risk of these events happening increases during or soon after exertion, in young people with congenital heart problems and adults with hidden or known coronary heart disease. However, evidence from a Seattle study shows that the benefits of regular exercise outweigh the risks for healthy subjects: men who spent less than 20 minutes per week exercising had a relative risk of exercise-related cardiac arrest that was 56 times greater than at rest, while men who spent more than 140 minutes per week exercising had a relative risk that was only five times greater than at rest. It is highly noteworthy that while the relative risk of cardiac arrest was greater during exercise than at rest, the total incidence of cardiac arrest, both at rest and during exercise, decreased with increasing physical activity levels. As a comparison, the total incidence of cardiac arrest in the least active group was 18 events per 1,000,000 person-hours, whereas in the most active group, it was only five per million person-hours.

Sedentarism is a major risk factor for cardiovascular disease, and exercise intervention is effective in managing cardiovascular risk factors as such as hypertension, diabetes/insulin resistance, hyperlipidaemia, obesity, as well as coronary artery disease itself.

In exercise-related sudden death, there is always a cause for the collapse of the victim. Sometimes, it is obvious (e.g. someone with a completely blocked coronary artery), and sometimes the cause is hard to identify even during autopsy (e.g. in sudden death due to an abnormality of the electrical conduction of the heart, the heart appears normal during autopsy). If there is no underlying abnormality in the heart then exercise, however intense, does not damage the heart. Hence, to prevent sudden death, the key is in identifying underlying heart disease through pre participation screening.

Pre-Participation Screening

General health screening is aimed at picking up common treatable conditions, such as diabetes, hypertension, high cholesterol, and early cancers. However, in sports, pre-participation screening or clearance is aimed more towards reducing the risk of injury or harm during strenuous exercise.

There are generally three main parts to a pre-participation screening:

1. Cardiovascular clearance, to identify underlying conditions that may cause sudden death
2. Musculoskeletal screening to identify injuries that need to be managed to prevent aggravation or to identify factors that may predispose the athlete to future injuries
3. Identifying factors that may limit performance, e.g. anaemia, drugs

Pre-participation screening can range from a simple self-administered questionnaire (e.g. Physical Activity Readiness Questionnaire, or PAR-Q) to a check-up by a doctor coupled with comprehensive tests such as a treadmill stress test and imaging of the heart. How comprehensive your pre-participation screening should be depends on your intrinsic risk factors and your level of participation. For example, if you are a healthy 25 year old who does not smoke, has a normal body mass index, exercises regularly, and has no family history of chronic diseases, then a PAR-Q would suffice. But if you are overweight, have been sedentary, and have a family history of heart disease or stroke, then a comprehensive pre-participation screening is recommended. Discuss with your sports physician to see what would be appropriate for you.

10. RUNNING GEAR

>>With input from William Chin, Malia Ho, Adam Jorgensen & Lim Baoying

Compared to other sports, running is a sport for 'purists,' as minimal equipment is involved. But having said that, there is still a huge variety of running products for us to choose from, ranging from socks to sophisticated training software.

A simple decision like picking a pair of running shorts can end up in painful chafing of the inner thighs during your run. So here are some simple tips when selecting your running gear.

RUNNING SHOES

As history tells us, the ancient Greeks ran barefoot (and naked) at the first Olympics. Unfortunately with the advent of modern pavements and our propensity to litter our environment with hazardous refuse, footwear has become a necessity for all, including runners.

Running shoes provide us with four main functions: (1) Most obviously, running shoes protect our feet against hazards on running surfaces as well as protection from the elements; (2) Cushioning has become one of the most desired functions. As most runners run on hard, unrelenting surfaces such as concrete and bitumen, the cushioning within the shoe is vital for protecting our entire body against the hazards of repetitive shock; (3) Stability is now recognised as an important function as runners become more aware of injuries associated with excessive motion within the foot; (4) Shoes provide a safe grip on the running surface.

In modern designs of shoes, all these four functions should be addressed in order to maintain good performance as well as prevent injury.

The Versatile Foot

To find the right shoes for you, let us first understand the foot and foot biomechanics. Our foot is made up of 26 bones held together by many ligaments and tendons. Our foot has the amazing capability of being a mobile adaptor at heel strike and yet switching to a rigid lever to allow for effective propulsion at heel lift/toe off. Here is what happens to our foot from foot strike to midstance to toe off:

1. At heel strike, the foot makes contact with the ground, usually on the outside of the heel (supination). As we transfer our bodyweight onto the foot, it rolls inwards (pronation) (see figure 10.1). This pronation unlocks the major joints in the foot, allowing the foot to be flexible enough to adapt to the uneven terrain that we run on. This movement also helps to absorb the shock generated by the landing foot.

2. At midstance, the foot is directly under the body and bears the full bodyweight. The foot is maximally pronated at this stage, and the heel is almost perpendicular to the ground (see figure 10.2). The heel may go beyond the vertical into slight pronation. Anything beyond a slight pronation is considered an over-pronated foot.

3. From midstance to toe off, the foot starts to re-supinate (see figure 10.3). Supination locks the joints in the foot making it a rigid lever to for pushing off.

Both pronation and supination are essential components of movement in the foot without which we would not be able to run efficiently and economically. Problems usually arise when there is excessive pronation or excessive supination in the foot.

Foot Types

Determining your foot type allows you understand how your foot functions and moves. It also provides you with good information of what type of injuries you may be more prone to so that you can take active steps to prevent them. These steps include focusing on certain groups of muscles when you do your warm ups, stretches and strengthening, as well as choosing the appropriate running footwear.

Pes Planus or Flat Feet. The arch of the foot may be deficient or absent in two ways: (1) Lax ligaments fail to hold up the joints in the midfoot, or (2) The arch may seem to disappear when the foot over-pronates. The first condition is rare and is usually seen in individuals with severe ligamentous laxity (loose ligaments that can result in joint instability). The second cause is more common. When the foot over-pronates, the heel everts (turns outwards), the arch flattens and the forefoot abducts/splays (turns outwards). Clinical features of a flat foot caused by over-pronation include everted heels, medial bulge in the midfoot (see figure 10.4), clawed/retracted toes, and loss of arch profile.

Figure 10.1 (top). The foot is supinated at foot strike. Figure 10.2 (middle). A maximally pronated foot at midstance. Figure 10.3 (bottom). The foot supinates at heel lift.

Runners with flat feet are susceptible to particular injuries, including plantar fasciitis, Achilles enthesiopathy and tendinopathy, medial tibial stress syndrome, and patellofemoral pain to name a few.

Pes Cavus Or High Arched Feet.   The arch of the foot is more prominent than usual, owing to certain neurological conditions that cause muscle imbalances and spasms that pull the arch up, or more commonly over-supination. The clinical features of a high arched feet include an inverted heel, elevated arch, and adducted forefoot (see figure 10.5).

When the foot over supinates or fails to pronate, it is rigid and thus does not conform well to uneven surfaces and absorbs shock poorly. This leads to certain injuries, including stress fractures, recurrent inversion ankle sprains, and iliotibial band friction syndrome.

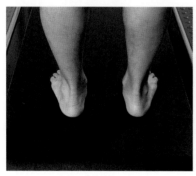

Figure 10.4 (left). Everted heels and medial bulge in the midfoot (arrows). Figure 10.5 (right). Inverted heels with high arch.

A rough gauge of your foot type would be your footprint. Simply wet your foot and step on the ground or on a piece of paper. If most of your arch area is in contact with the ground, you probably have flat feet. Conversely, if little of your arch is seen, then you probably with high arched feet. If you are in- between, then you have a normal arch. (see figure 10.6).

Figure 10.6. Footprints indicating (from left) flat foot, high arched foot and normal foot.

Footprints remain a poor gauge of foot type, as the actual height of the arch is not captured effectively on a footprint. It would be like trying to determine the height of a building by measuring its floor area! Many tools and indices have been devised to try to determine exactly where the boundaries are between the foot types but none have been very successful. Furthermore, it is common for the feet to look normal when standing, and over-pronate on running due to the increased loading. Similarly, a pressure map of the bottom of the feet does not necessarily give an accurate reading of the feet's function. Hence, it is best to see your sports podiatrist or sports physician to assess you while running on a treadmill (e.g. video gait analysis), in order to get a more functional assessment.

Optimizing Foot Function During Running

Interventions for pes planus and cavus include selecting the appropriate shoe type and/or getting fitted with orthoses (shoe inserts). In mild cases, selecting the right shoe would suffice.

The figures below show the same runner wearing two designs of shoes. He is over-pronating in the first pair of shoes (figure 10.7a) but not the second ones (figure 10.7b) which provide more support and stability. Therefore, the best and probably most accurate way to determine your foot type would be to consult your sports physician or sports podiatrist who will observe you standing, walking and running.

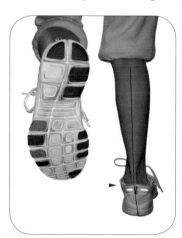 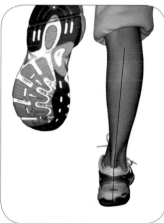

Figure 10.7a (left) & 10.7b (right). These two photos show the same runner wearing two designs of shoes. On the left (10.7a), the left foot is over-pronating, with a medial bulge at the midfoot (arrow). On the right (10.7b), with the appropriate shoes, the foot is neutral and no longer over-pronates.

If the shoe type fails to correct the abnormal biomechanics, then your podiatrist may be able to rectify the problem using functional foot orthoses. Foot orthoses are devices that are placed in the shoe to support and correct the function of the foot. Orthoses for over-pronators include features such as medial heel and forefoot wedges plus arch supports (see figure 10.8b). If a runner over-supinates, the foot orthoses would need to provide sufficient cushioning for a rigid foot, and will have features such as heel cushions and paddings. Off-the-shelf orthoses may be adequate for mild cases, but customized ones are recommended for moderate to severe cases. A more detailed discussion follows in the next section (pages 190 – 192).

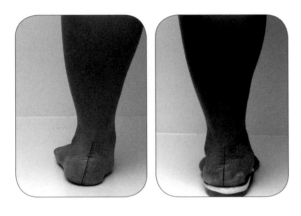

Figure 10.8 a (left) & 10 b (right). An over-pronated foot without an orthotic (10.8a), and the same over-pronated foot supported by a foot orthotic (10.8b).

Anatomy of the Shoe

The shoe last is a wooden, aluminium or plastic 3D form upon which the shoe materials are sewn, moulded and glued onto to develop its final shape. The shape of the last has been

Figure. 10.9. Parts of a running shoe. Each shoe has an upper (comprising the heel counter, vamp, and toe box) and a sole (comprising the insole, midsole, and outsole).

Heel Counter

Midsole

Vamp

Toe box

Outer sole

thought to contribute in some way to the stability of the shoe — an unstable, over-pronating foot needs a straight-lasted shoe, whereas a supinated foot needs a curve-lasted shoe. However, the last shape is probably more relevant to the shape of these feet rather than their contribution to stability.

A shoe is made up of several parts (see figure 10.9). The 'heart' of the shoe is the midsole. This is where the majority of the shoes' cushioning and stability are incorporated and hence the majority of research has been focused. Modern running shoe midsoles are made from ethyl vinyl acetate (EVA) or similar proprietary variations of EVA, providing a good mix of cushioning and durability.

Shoe Types

Running shoes can be designed for training or performance. Training shoes are for the majority who run for fun or fitness. Training shoes comprise trail, motion control, stability, or cushioning shoes.

Trail shoes are primarily meant for off-road running. Their most obvious feature is the rugged looks topped off with the prominent lugs on the outsole for best grip in muddy or rocky terrains. These shoes tend to have heavier and sturdier uppers (the cloth or canvas above the sole of the shoe) to assist in stabilising the unpredictable footfalls that often occur on rough terrain. Waterproofing is also sometimes added into the upper. Combined with the heavy outsole, the weight of trail shoes tends to be more than the regular training shoes. Most brands do not offer much variation in functional types as their training cousins do.

Motion control, stability, and cushioning represent a functional spectrum suited for foot types ranging from over-pronators to under-pronators (supinators). Depending on whether you have a flat, neutral, or high arch, there are shoes designed for each foot type:

Shoe Type	Motion Control	Stability	Cushioning
Foot Type:	Over-Pronator	Neutral	Under-Pronator
Features:	• Good longitudingal stability • Dual-density midsole • Plug of plastic on the inner side of the midsole • Generally straight-lasted	• Fairly good longitudinal stability • Dual-density midsole • The increase in bulk and density of the midsole adds to the shoe weight • Semi-curved last	• Thick midsole made from low-density EVA or similar proprietary variations for cushioning • Addition of special shock absorbent materials (e.g. air bags, silicon gels and honeycomb matrices) for durability and weight reduction • Often curve-lasted to follow the natural foot curvature of the high-arched foot

Performance shoes comprise racing, spike, and triathlon shoes. Racing shoes are primarily for those running at elite, competitive levels. These are ultra lightweight shoes that minimise weight at the end of the limbs and reduce the energy cost of running. Much of the weight is discarded by eliminating much of the heavy midsole cushioning and stability systems. Some reduction may also be achieved using thinner and lighter fabrics in the upper and lacing. The down side is the loss of cushioning, stability and durability. Hence, if you are carrying excess weight, new to running, or have impact injuries from running, it is best to avoid using them.

Racing spikes are usually only worn in track events, but occasionally worn in cross-country racing. The spike plate is usually only on the forefoot as it is assumed that at the race speeds, majority of the load is borne by the forefoot.

With speciality events comes the advent of specialty shoes. Triathlon running is unique as it requires the runner to put on his/her shoes rapidly and are often worn with wet feet and without socks. Features unique to these shoes are the drainage points and quick fix lacing systems. The upper is usually seamless to avoid any blistering, as the runner is sockless.

Selecting a Running Shoe

Shoe preferences and suitability differ between individuals. There are many brands and models to choose from, and it's not always true that the more costly shoe is the better shoe for you. To decide if a shoe is suitable for you, put it through these four simple steps:

1. Squeeze the heel counter between your thumb and fingers to see if it is firm and to ensure the sides do not collapse easily (see figure 10.10). This is especially relevant if you are an over-pronator, as you need a firm heel counter to hold your heels.

2. Rotate the shoe along its long axis and ensure that the shank is rigid (see figure 10.11). A shank that twists easily allows the midfoot to produce extraneous motion. A rigid mid section is helpful in those with pes planus or prone to plantar fasciitis.

3. Push the two ends of the shoe together, between your hands (see figure 10.12). This assesses the location and flexibility of the toe break. The toe break should correspond to where the ball of your foot is when inside the shoe. Those with pain at the joint of the big toe (hallux rigidus) or plantar fasciitis should go for a shoe with a stiffer toe break.

4. The length of the shoe should be such that there is a thumb's width in front of your toes (see figure 10.13). Ensure that the shoe is the right size and width, and feels comfortable. Sizing in footwear varies slightly between manufacturers. Similarly, two different models in the same shoe brand may have a sizing difference. Always fit shoes standing up, as the foot elongates in weight bearing. A shoe which is too short may lead to the toes striking the end of the shoe while running, resulting in black nails. Apart from the length, be sure that the forefoot width fits as well. Check the width by pinching the material of the upper with the fingers across the ball of the foot — you should be

able to gather a small amount of upper only. Too little, and the shoe may squeeze the forefoot resulting in blisters or pinching of the forefoot nerves; too much and the shoe becomes unstable and sloppy in the forefoot. Shoes with a narrower width are indicated by the number of the letter 'A', with 'AA' being narrower than 'A.' The wide versions are indicated by 'W', 'WW', and so on.

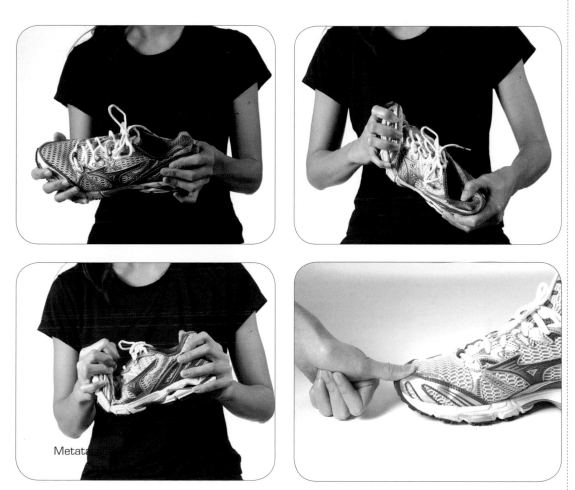

Top row left to right: Figure 10.10 & 10.11 Bottom row left to right: Figure 10.12 & 10.13. Selecting a runnng shoe. Figure 10.10. Squeeze the heel counter to assess its firmness. Figure 10.11. Twist the long axis of the shoe to assess the rigidity of the shank. Figure 10.12. Push the two ends together to assess the metatarsal break. Figure 10.13. Ensure a thumb's width in front of the toes for proper fit.

For further comfort, there are various lacing techniques to better secure the rearfoot, relieve pressure areas on the top of the foot, and to accommodate forefoot deformities such as bunions.

Ultimately, the most important aspect of fitting shoes is comfort. The proof of the pudding is in the eating, so try out the shoes by walking around in them. Breaking in new shoes is a must. A slow build-up in mileage in the shoe will season both the feet and the shoe.

HOW LONG DO RUNNING SHOES LAST ?

Traditionally running shoes are usually quoted as lasting around 800 km. How was this number arrived at? Well it was found that for the average 75 kg male, the number of cycles (loading and unloading on EVA) that he would go through before the midsole lost 50 per cent of its memory was extrapolated to be around 800 km.

Factors that will accelerate the degradation are exposure to moisture, heat and humidity, the amount of load, and frequency of use. Even when a shoe sits on the shelf, the EVA deteriorates over time and loses its resilience and cushioning. So change your shoes when they have covered about 800 km or when they are approximately six to 12 months old. Do not wait till the outsole has worn out, as some outsole materials outlast the midsole.

ORTHOSES

What are Orthoses?

A common method of addressing biomechanical abnormalities or dysfunction is through the use of foot orthoses (also called arch supports, insoles, foot orthotics), which are devices placed inside footwear or directly on the foot, to improve function of the foot and lower limb.

How do Foot Orthoses Work?

Foot orthoses alter the function of the feet by applying forces to various areas of the foot to change the type of motion that occurs in the feet. Orthoses are usually used to change abnormal, excessive motion in the feet that could be the cause of abnormal stress in the tissues of the feet, legs, hips or back.

As stated previously the enemies of running shoes are exposure to moisture, heat and humidity, salt from the sweat, the amount of load, and frequency of use. Minimise all these situations by drying out your shoes after running. Stuff with newspaper to wick out the moisture. Air dry only. Do not place in heat, sun, oven, or dryer.

Have two or more pairs to swap and allow 48 hours recovery — this may extend the shoes' life beyond 800 km.

Types of Orthoses

The three most common types are:

- **Prefabricated.** These include arch supports, wedges, pads, cushions etc., and are usually readily available in pharmacies, shoe stores, sports stores and even supermarkets. They should be cheap and easy to fix into shoes and are usually the first line of home care treatment.

- **Customised.** These devices are basically pre-fabricated insoles that are then modified in some way to tailor to a runner's feet and needs. Modifications may include heel lifts, added cushioning, wedging, arch fill and softer covers. These are more technical than the plain prefabricated ones, and are often suitable for runners needing more significant support that the prefabricated ones alone cannot provide.

- **Custom Made.** These are the most technical devices and hence require the most effort, training, patience and money to dispense. These are usually reserved for those whose feet and or biomechanics are so far from the norm, that the customized devices do not provide adequate effect (see figure 10.14). They are usually made from a mould of the feet after careful biomechanical evaluation. The moulds are then used as the template on which the foot orthoses raw materials are moulded. The whole process could take between two days to a week. It will take you about a week to get accustomed to using your new orthose, so it is good to schedule your visit with the sports podiatrist at least three months before your race. While custom made are tailored from the exact shape of the feet, their biomechanical effect is much more aggressive and has the potential to cause problems instead of fixing problems.

Figure 10.14. Custom made functional orthoses

Do I need Foot Orthoses?

Not all flat-footed runners will have problems. In fact, most of the African runners tend to have flat appearing feet, as do many other racers.

For most patients there are really only two instances where foot orthoses are recommended. Firstly, when the runner is suffering from pain. Foot orthoses may be used in the treatment and subsequent prevention of pain provided that the abnormal biomechanics has played a role in the symptoms or their delayed resolution. If the symptoms are due to overtraining, then simply correcting the biomechanics will rarely suffice. Secondly, foot orthoses are indicated in the management of significant deformity. In the presence of significant deformity, abnormal biomechanical forces have the potential to exacerbate the deformity leading to an increase in abnormal and deforming forces. These forces then have the potential to cause pain and lasting tissue damage.

Which Type Should I Use?

As a general guide, the more abnormal the biomechanics and the deformity, then the more technical the foot orthosis required. Or start with the simple, cheap option first, and then work your way up.

CLOTHING

Running apparel can differ in the fabric type, design and of course, cost. Current running apparel focuses on the use of "high-tech" material, each with its purported advantages. What they have in common is that they are designed to pull, or wick, moisture away from your body, to dry quickly, and to be lightweight and stretchable. In contrast, the typical cotton t-shirt retains and traps sweat, which not only weighs the runner down, but also hinders heat dissipation.

Running Tops

Women, take note — 80 per cent of you wear the wrong sports bra size. Try on three sizes — the cup size you normally wear, one that's smaller, and one that's larger, as the bra fit differs from brand to brand. Straps should not gape, dig into the skin, or move around. The base band should feel snug and lie flat all the way around. You should be able to slide two fingers under each strap and one finger under the base band on each side, the front, and the back. If the bra's material wrinkles or gathers anywhere, the bra is too big. If your skin bulges out in spots or if the edges cut into you, the bra is too small.

Look for seams with rolled edges and off-centre stitching to minimize chafing. To reduce bouncing, look for a bra that encapsulates each breast into a distinct cup.

Put the bra on, and clap your hands over your head. If the band of the bra slides up your torso, it is too tight. Run in place for 10 – 15 seconds or hop on a treadmill if available. You should feel supported and the bra should not twist or ride up while you move.

Wash the bra in cold water with powder detergent, since liquids clog fabric pores, which inhibit moisture wicking. Tumble dry on low or let it air dry to prolong the life of the elastic. After about 72 washes, when the elastic starts to lose resilience, or if your weight changes, you should replace the bra.

For men, it is easier. Get a top that is comfortable, especially around the chest and armholes. The material should be light, with good wicking properties. When racing in warm, tropical climates, less is best.

Compression Garments

Compression garments, though costly, are getting popular. The purported benefits for runners are:

- Lower blood lactate concentrations following maximal exercise.

- Achieves optimal skin and muscle temperature — compression garments are thought to decrease warm-up time and raise the muscle temperature to the optimal 38.5°C and maintain the skin/muscle temperature, thereby enhancing muscle performance. Additionally, it is thought that increased musculotendinous temperature may reduce injury potential. It is uncertain whether these claims remain valid in warm climates.

- Enhanced athletic performance (specifically, repetitive jump power) has been demonstrated with compressive garments, and possible mechanisms include a reduction in muscle oscillation, improved proprioception (position awareness), and increased resistance to fatigue. Additionally, it has been shown that the added opposing resistance against contracting muscles due to a compressive garment does not impede muscle performance.

- The elasticity of the compression garment is thought to provide recoil at the end of the range of motion of the limbs.

- Draws moisture away from the skin.

- UV protection.

What To Wear For Temperate Marathons

For most, running a marathon in about 15 – 20°C would be most comfortable — all you need to wear is a light running singlet and shorts. But cold tolerance varies between individuals, so if unsure, dress in layers so that you can shed the outer layers just before or after the start of the race.

Some marathons are run in colder temperatures, and even if you have registered for a race in temperatures that are expected to be in the teens, do go prepared for rain and colder temperatures, as the weather is not always predictable. Most race organisers' websites will provide the expected temperature range, historical race temperatures, or weather updates leading up to the race. With regards to the latter, do check the race websites before departing for the race, as they may provide the latest storm warnings.

Runners who are born, bred, and trained in tropical climates do not have to be apprehensive of running in temperate climates. Runners from cold climates and racing in warmer locales have to acclimatise to the heat; whereas runners from hot climates do not have to acclimatise to the cold, as long as they know how to dress for their trip and race. When racing in colder weather, always remember:

- Dress in layers, so that outer layers can be added/shed easily
- Stay dry — when clothes get soaked, you get cold

Here is a guide on how to dress in layers, for the start of the race:

Temp range (°C)	Number of layers						
	Inner	Outer	Shell	Tights	Gloves	Hat	Socks
10 to 15	1	0	0	1	1	0	1
5 to 10	1	1	0	1	1	0	1
1 to 5	1	1	0	1 – 2	1	1	1
-10 to 0	1	1	1	2	1	1	1
-20 to -10	1	1	1	pants	1	1	1

- **Inner layer.** The layer closest to the skin should be a skin-tight, lightweight fabric that wicks water away from the skin. Tops should be long-sleeved and skin-tight (without chafing). Alternatively, you can use removable sleeves.

- **Outer layer.** The next layer should be a looser, medium weight fabric that wicks water. A zipper at the neck is convenient for temperature control. An old t-shirt is a cheap option if you intend to shed it during the race.

- **Shell.** A waterproof or water resistant shell that is breathable is useful in the coldest conditions, to protect from wind, rain and cold. Gore-tex is considered the best fabric, but there are cheaper alternatives.

- **Tights.** Used as inner or outer layers. Lycra tights of various thickness are available, depending on the temperature.

- **Gloves.** Any cotton glove works. There are wind-resistant ones that provide more protection. If you are from a warm climate, it is likely that your fingers will not tolerate the cold well, so a good pair of gloves would be useful.

- **Hat or headgear.** A lot of heat is lost through the scalp, so a beanie or hat is a must for most people. Cotton hats get too heavy with sweat. Balaclavas are more versatile than hats, and allow you to cover your neck/face if requires.

- **Socks.** A wicking sock will seem less heavy and keep your feet drier than a conventional sock would.

If travelling from a warm to cold climate to race, do arrive early enough to do at least one run before the race to try out how many layers you will need for the start of the race. Often, the wait for the start can be quite a while, so it is important to stay warm and comfortable during this time. Some runners even bring a disposable blanket to wrap themselves with while waiting. During the race, as your muscles generate heat, you will likely need to shed the outer layers. For the layers you are expected to shed, there are usually cheap options, e.g. simple cotton gloves and plastic ponchos.

ELECTRONIC GADGETS

The very elite do not wear foot pods or heart rate monitors during races, because they have been running a long time and have very good feel of their pace and heart rate. During training, their coaches have a stop watch on hand to record their timings for them. Less experienced runners and runners who do not have the luxury of a coach can do with some help in the form of electronic aids. There are lots of fun electronic gadgets in the market to help you train and race better.

Watch

This is a must-have. Look for an electronic watch that has the following features: Lightweight, durable, water-resistant, a display that is easy to read, backlight (some races start before sunrise), buttons that are easy to activate but do not get depressed accidentally, a stop watch function with lots of split time memory, and a count-down timer that can be programmed to beep at fixed intervals. The last feature is useful for pacing yourself during a race and for interval training.

Heart Rate Monitors

We run at different speeds or intensities for different purposes, e.g. intervals, tempo runs, pace runs, long runs. The most convenient way to monitor your exercise intensity is to wear a heart rate monitor. This comprises a chest strap holding a device that picks up your heart rate by detecting electrical currents from your heart, and a receiver embedded in a wristwatch.

A good heart rate monitor picks up your heart rate accurately (i.e. no missing signals despite running vigorously) and is immune to cross talk with other runners' heart rate monitors (this is especially important as you will be running in close proximity with other runners wearing heart rate monitors during a race). Very useful functions to look for are heart rate limits and calorie counters. The former allows you to set upper and lower heart rate limits so that the watch beeps to let you know whether you are running too fast or too slow from your intended intensity. The calorie counter is a must for those who want to manage their weight, as it gives a good indication of energy expended during exercise so that you can plan your diet accordingly to achieve a set daily calorie deficit (see Chapter 7).

Other functions that come with the more sophisticated models include wireless downloading of heart rate data onto your desktop, together with software to chart your training, gauge your fatigue levels, estimate your fitness levels, etc. There are models that are coupled with accelerometers or global positioning systems, to provide an integrated training solution.

Accelerometers

The accelerometer, as the name implies, measures acceleration, and from this, the running speed, distance, and cadence can be computed. The pager-sized device, called a foot pod, is attached to the top of the shoe. As you run, it picks up the acceleration of your foot with each step and transmits it to the wristwatch. As the runner's gait and cadence changes with the running speed, the accelerometer has to be calibrated for various speeds. The calibration involves running a fixed distance at a steady pace. The data is less reliable if the training or race speed is not kept relatively constant, e.g. during trail running.

As there are moving parts in the accelerometer to detect motion, durability is a problem. Do get a model that is robust yet lightweight.

Global Positioning System

The global positioning system (GPS) has shrunk to the size of what looks like a bulky wristwatch! It helps to track the distance covered and provides almost real-time running speed. It even gives you information about your ascents and descents during your runs. With most models, the data can even be downloaded onto your desktop computer, churning out charts of your training mileages and running performance.

The catch is that tree cover and tall buildings can block GPS signals. So if you are running in a dense forest or a city packed with skyscrapers, the readings may not be reliable.

Other Motion Sensors

Instead of an accelerometer, Nike has a simpler motion sensor that only detects movement (unable to measure acceleration). The sensor is much smaller and lighter than an accelerometer, and it is inserted under the insole of a Nike Plus enabled shoe (i.e. shoes with a recess in the midsole for the sensor). With each movement detected, it sends a signal to a receiver, which can be in a wristwatch or in the ipod Nano. In other words, it picks up the number of steps that you take, and this gives a rough estimate of the distance covered (without considering the stride length).

Nike Plus records your distance, speed, and calories. An online community feature allows the user to set up challenges and virtual track meets with other nikeplus.com users, and even chart the progress of all Nike users around the world.

RESPIRATORY TRAINING AIDS

Altitude training, when done correctly, has been found to improve endurance performance. The low-oxygen environment stimulates the production of red blood cells in the body, thus improving oxygen-carrying capacity and performance when racing at lower altitudes.

But travelling to a high altitude training camp for two or more weeks is not practical for many, so 'nitrogen houses' have been built and are used instead. These are basically rooms where nitrogen is pumped in to displace oxygen, thereby simulating the low-oxygen atmosphere at high altitudes. The amount of nitrogen pumped in can be adjusted to simulate various altitudes. Athletes sleep or train in such rooms to improve their aerobic capacities. However, such facilities are also very costly. The practical alternatives come in the form of nitrogen tents or the hypoxicator.

Hypoxicator

The hypoxicator is a portable device that intermittently delivers air that is reduced in oxygen content to the athlete. This lowers the oxygen levels in the blood, stimulating a compensatory increase in red blood cells. A pulse-oximeter monitors the oxygen level in the blood to ensure that it does not dip to dangerously low levels while using the hypoxicator. The athlete uses the equipment for about half an hour a day (the prescription varies), daily. You can purchase or rent the hypoxicator, or you can go to a facility to use the hypoxicator.

Inspiratory Muscle Trainers

During the dash for the finishing line, or during interval training, we have all felt what it is like to be short of air. At high exercise intensities, we hyperventilate and activate our accessory muscles of respiration (e.g. the neck muscles), in addition to activating our diaphragmatic and intercostals muscles, to suck in more air. It is thought that by training these muscles, we become more efficient at breathing, even at moderate exercise intensities.

Like other muscles, these accessory muscles can be trained by making them work against resistance. In this case, the resistance is provided by a simple handheld device that restricts the airflow as we inhale through it. An example is the POWERbreathe trainer. It comes with training instructions and claims noticeable differences after using daily for three weeks.

11. AMAZING OVERSEAS MARATHONS -CUM-HOLIDAYS

>>With input from Ben Swee

Marathons are not only about challenging ourselves, but also experiencing the world! I have long grown tired of being a typical tourist touring the city on a sightseeing bus. Now, I make it a point to go for a run in every city that I visit and combine my holidays with a marathon or trek, to add a special dimension to each trip. Imagine running up to the Parthenon in Athens in the wee hours of the mornings, with hardly a tourist in sight, and soaking in the sunrise! Or jogging along the rugged mountain slopes of Bhutan at an altitude of 3,000 m, awed by the snow-capped Himalayas! Or braving the -15°C temperatures while jogging along the water's edge in Helsinki! Or being amidst the flora and fauna of the Amazon as you jog through the trails of Rio de Janeiro's national parks! As a marathoner, you have worked hard to cumulatively attain a level of fitness that most people do not have — make use of your hard-earned fitness to experience the world in an extraordinary way.

There are countless marathons in every corner of the world, from the Great Wall of China to Antarctica where you'll run "in thick snow, high winds and in between human sized penguins," recounts Matt Chapman, who ran the Racing the Planet series. My personal aim is to do an overseas marathon a year, a different one each time. Coupled with the Singapore Marathon, that makes it two marathons a year, giving my body adequate time to recover and train between marathons.

For serious runners, there are the five Marathon Majors that many aim to participate in, so as to complete a personal 'grand slam.' These are the Boston, Berlin, London, Chicago, and New York Marathons. Many runners dream of making a 'pilgrimage' to Boston to run the world's oldest marathon — if they can meet the tough qualification time. Berlin, the fastest marathon course on earth, has seen a few world records being set on its course, and is the perennial favourite of those aiming to set their personal best marathon time. When Haile Gabrselassie set the current world record time of 2:03:59 in the 2008 Berlin marathon, I was there running on the very same course, albeit finishing a whole hour behind him.

For those looking to experience unique scenery and cultures, there is an even longer list to pick from. The following list is a small sampling of what the marathon world has to offer. Apart from the Marathon Majors, we have included mostly nearby marathons and a few not-so-near but must-try marathons in our list of recommended marathons.

When racing overseas, do remember to pack the appropriate clothing, arrive approximately three days before the race, adjust to the local time, do a light practice run two days before the race, familiarise yourself with certain stretches of the course, check the weather details, and finally get adequate sleep before the race.

MARATHON/ COUNTRY/ MONTH	WHY YOU HAVE TO GIVE IT A TRY

Boston Marathon
(World Marathon Major)
USA
April

The Boston Marathon is the world's oldest annual marathon and ranks as one of the most prestigious events in the world. Participants must meet a qualification time based on their age group at a certified marathon in order to qualify. The route is hilly, with the notorious 'Heartbreak Hill' being one of them. Awesome crowd, great organisation, and excellent race expo make this a race you should try at least once in your lifetime.

"I'll always remember the Boston Marathon, for the race itself and for the fact that I had to work hard to qualify for it. I failed to meet the qualification time of 3:15 at the Melbourne Marathon, and only made it on my second attempt, at the Ohtawara Marathon (Japan) with a time of 3:14:59! Boston itself was tough — Heartbreak Hill wasn't the only one causing me heartbreak, as there were many hills before and after that, and even the finish was uphill. As a hurricane had just passed through, we were running in 4 – 8 °C, rain, and 50 km/h winds."
— Ben Tan, who finished the 2007 Boston Marathon in 3:19:04

Berlin Marathon
(World Marathon Major)
Germany
September

Touted as the fastest marathon course in the world, it promises a fantastic race atmosphere with more than 1 million supporters and 70 live bands along a flat route. It brings runners alongside many of Berlin's famous landmarks and passes under the majestic Brandenburg Gate towards the finishing line.

"I enjoy the Berlin Marathon, having run the race twice already. The course is fast and the weather was perfect, and best of all, I got to meet and take a photo with my running idol, Haile Gabrselassie, the current world record holder! Berlin is the place for breaking records, and it feels really inspiring to have run in the very same marathon where Haile broke his own world record to set a new record of 2:03:59 in 2008! I was honoured to be part of marathon history, where the first man ran under 2:04"
— Daniel Ling, winner of the 2007 Singapore Marathon (local men's category)

London Marathon
(World Marathon Major)
United Kingdom
April

With a fairly flat course allowing for fast marathon timings and the support of 1 million spectators, it attracts athletes from more than 50 countries each year. A first class event with great organisation, running past famous landmarks such as Big Ben, with a memorable finish in front of Buckingham Palace. Due to the overwhelming response each year, entry is by balloting — you may not get a place on your first try.

"This is by far the most memorable and enjoyable marathon of all, having done 4 out of the 5 World Majors. I ran it 3 times and each one offered a different experience. One year it was the hottest day in London Marathon history and another year it was the wettest and coldest race. In 2004, I ran a PB in 3.21.30 making it the most challenging one. The course itself is flat with a slight incline on to Tower Bridge at 12.5 miles mark. There has been an improvement on the course – instead of running on the cobblestones along the Embankment, the organiser has shifted the route onto the cement surface, making it a much faster race. There was never a dull moment weaving round London's famous tourist sights and the continuous support of the million visitors making the run so much fun."
— JJ Shepherd, an active member of Singapore's running community, finished the 2007 edition in 3.22.33 and placed 6th for her age group

Chicago Marathon
(World Marathon Major)
USA
October

Chicago is a one-loop course that is flat, wide and fast. It starts and finishes in the vast expanse of Grant Park on the shores of Lake Michigan, and showcases many of Chicago's attractions — from the city-centre skyscrapers to the diverse ethnic neighbourhoods that most tourists never see. Crowd support is excellent, giving you endless cheers to accompany you through the marathon that has a cut-off time of 6hr 30mins.

"Even though I've since had several other equally amazing and memorable marathon experiences elsewhere, Chicago 2002 remains the big sentimental favourite for me, perhaps also because it was my first overseas 'big race.' I was totally blown away by the tremendous crowd support and carnival atmosphere of the entire race. It was a freezing 5°C or so at the early morning start (I wore two tops, gloves, a fleece head band) and here were all these people (who could or should well still be snug in bed at that hour) who were out there on the sidewalks, armed with posters, banners and all sorts of things to make noise with, cheering us on. It was one marathon that I truly totally enjoyed! My run time wasn't anything

New York City Marathon
(World Marathon Major)
USA
November

One of the world's largest spectator presence lines the route of this challenging marathon that is filled with slopes. You are guaranteed an energetic race atmosphere along a course that will have you running through the beautiful city sights and finishing in the vast Central Park. The race expo is a shoppers' paradise for runners. Be prepared for the cold while awaiting the start and for the large crowd of fellow runners.

"Of all the marathon majors that I have taken part in (Boston, New York & Berlin), I would place the New York City Marathon as a 'must-do' race for all runners. The atmosphere was awesome and electrifying. From start to finish, I was never on my own (and I am not referring to my fellow runners) — there were supporters lining the streets cheering runners on. It was like the whole of New York City was out there in their deck chairs, having breakfast, bringing out their pom-poms and cheerleaders. Besides these enthusiastic supporters, there were about 100 bands lined up along the way, playing and singing the latest musical hits — from rock bands to jazz groups to school bands — they were all out there in droves, entertaining us while we 'struggled' to keep up the spirit. And all of them did it as volunteers! And these were not your 'run-of-the-mill' wannabes — the quality of their music would have had me stopping in my tracks to dance and sing along with them! When I do run the NYC Marathon again, the camera will definitely be an item to bring along — a PB will be a secondary consideration! Weather-wise it was cold at the start as we had to wait for a while but once the gun went off, so did all the warm clothing and there were enough discards to provide for the needy during winter! The NYC Marathon is a great chance to see the city without having to engage a tour agent, as the route will take you through all its 5 boroughs within those few hours — Staten Island, Brooklyn, Queens, Bronx and Manhattan. One other significant feature of the NYC Marathon is the Friendship Run the day before. This event is reserved for international runners only (with a few exceptions for some US runners). Participants come in their national costumes and gather at the UN building for a 5km run and the event is indeed friendly and relaxed. It would be great to get a big group of Singaporeans to run at a NYC Marathon and

create our own version of a national costume representing our rojak community, we might just stand out among the international colours."

— David Tay, an avid marathoner who aims to complete the
Marathon Majors soon

Prague International Marathon
Czech Republic
May

This is a marathon with a special appeal because of the stunning city. This fast course is also one of the most beautiful in the world. Since its inception in 1995, the Prague International Marathon has caught the attention of the rest of the world, with foreign entries making up the majority of the runners.

"Along the course, the enchanting sights took my mind off the pain and fatigue as we ran along the Vltava River. I was motivated to push on as I was looking forward to crossing the famous Charles Bridge (Karluv Most) towards the historic city. When we got into Old Town for the finishing line, my feet started hurting even more as we were running on cobblestone streets! The pain didn't last, but the memories of running a marathon in such a historic city certainly did."

— Ben Tan, finishing the 2004 edition in 3:45

Venice Marathon
Italy
October

Venice is worth going to just to see the historic city itself, and with its relatively flat and fast marathon course, your reasons for making a trip there is even more compelling. Temperatures are usually in the low teens. The first half of the race is in a typical countryside landscape, following the course of the river in the "Riviera del Brenta," before coursing through boroughs of the city of Venice, Europe's largest urban green, a 4-km bridge, the Venice port area and finishing in the city centre.

"I ran the Venice Marathon a couple of years ago. It starts outside Venice and ends in Venice itself. It's a beautiful finish with surrounding waters and gondolas. You can go for a gondola ride after the run to relax!"

— Vivian Tang, Singapore's top female marathoner

Stockholm Marathon
Sweden
June

The Stockholm Marathon started in 1979. With an unusual start time of 2 PM on a Saturday afternoon, this 2-lap scenic course takes you through the city centre, running along waterways, passing beautiful landmarks such as the Royal Palace, City Hall, Royal Opera and Houses of Parliament, starting and finishing at the Olympic Stadium. This is not a fast course due to some undulating terrain but the atmosphere is fantastic with a large crowd thronging the streets and superb volunteers. Cold drinks and many hoses are set up to cool runners.

"If you're not out to do a PB, the Stockholm marathon is a great way to sight-see and tour this gorgeous city. You cut through the town centre and beyond, past the big sights, some parks, lush greens and the city's sparklingly blue waterways, and cross a couple of bridges — and do it all twice, as it's a two-loop course. Best of all, perhaps, you start and end at Stockholm's historic Olympic Stadium, site of the 1912 Games. The 2PM start on a June Saturday can make for a fairly hot run, but the scene I seem to recall most out of the Stockholm Marathon is that of the amazingly blue sky and blue waters around the city. For me, it's one of the most scenic marathons I've done."

— Anna Teo, who participated in the 2003 Stockholm marathon
while still on a post-Chicago Marathon high

Walt Disney World Marathon
Orlando, Florida,
USA
January

It is a perfect way to see Disney World and run at the same time. Make sure that you sign up for the Goofy Challenge, which is a half marathon on Saturday, and a full marathon on Sunday. The route will take you through the theme parks of Disney World, with the Disney characters lined up along the route. A Donald Duck medal awaits finishers of the half marathon, and a Mickey Mouse medal for the full marathoners. Goofy Challengers will get an additional Goofy Medal. Make sure that you register online early as all the 3,000 places fill within days.

"The unique medals are worth every 63 km of pounding!"
— Mohanadas Kandiah, finisher of 71 marathons

Honolulu Marathon
USA
December

Held next to the ocean, it promises a very scenic run. Coupled with the vociferous crowd (lots of Japanese), enthusiastic volunteers and fireworks display at the start of the run, you are assured of a fantastic race atmosphere. The early start time at 5AM, generous provision of cold Gatorade and ice-cold wet sponges helps ward off the heat. Do be prepared to walk a fair bit after you finish before you can collect the finisher t-shirt and well-earned medal.

"Possibly one of the most fun-filled marathons that I have participated in. The camaraderie amongst the runners (mostly Japanese) was superb! It is a totally relaxed run that takes runners along a stretch of gentle rolling hills and past the

famous Diamond Head. Unfortunately, it is on the second Sunday in December —
a week after our Singapore's Standard Chartered Marathon. Book flights early, as
the Japan/Korea/Taiwan to Honolulu route is always full."

— Mohanadas Kandiah, finisher of 71 marathons

Nagano Marathon
Japan
April

The annual Nagano Olympic Commemorative Marathon commemorates the 1998
Nagano Winter Olympic Games. Participants run along some excellent facilities
that were used during the Nagano Olympics, finishing at the Olympic Memorial
Stadium. The weather is mild and the course is flat.

*"The race is very well organised — they have English-speaking guides ready to help
and foreign runners have priority queues for tag collection. The route is great —
imagine running through farms of apple trees, snow-capped alps in the distance,
and most importantly the cherry blossoms in full bloom! They provided really good
sports drinks and gave out palatable energy jelly. The best thing was the very
professional sports massage at the end, topped with icing and heat treatment if
needed!"*

— Dr Benny Goh, finishing the 2009 edition in a personal best time of 2:52:55

**Ohtawara
Marathon**
Japan
November

This is a scenic countryside marathon with a very local (i.e. non-commercial) touch.
Just two hours north of Tokyo by bullet train, the course is a relatively flat double-loop,
and the weather is practically guaranteed to be mild. This is a good race to try if you
are attempting a personal best or to qualify for Boston Marathon. After the race,
book yourself into a ryokan in the nearby Shiobara onsen district, and enjoy a heavenly
post-race dip in the hotspring! Could life get any better?

*"Ohtawara Marathon is held on the 23rd of Nov every year (Labour Thanksgiving
Day). It is one of the fastest courses, although a bit monotonous. Since the cut-off
time is 4 hours, there are only around 1,000 participants, so it is easy to run. The
10 km race is held at the same time. The free pork miso soup post-race is
delicious and will warm you up. (It may be quite chilly this time in this area.)
Definitely worth visiting the Shiobara Onsen hot-spring near by after the race —
you can enjoy the best season for coloured leaves in the mountains. Also a good
idea to get to Nikko and stay for a few days to visit its World Heritage Site of great
temples and shrines."*

— Mika Kume, a seasoned marathoner and triathlete based in Singapore

Gold Coast Marathon
Australia
July

Fantastic flat and scenic coastal route with a generous cut-off time of 7hr 10mins and enthusiastic supporters, especially those decked out in pyjamas. The start of the marathon is very orderly without pushing or shoving. Water stations are plentiful.

"The Gold Coast Airport Marathon holds fond memories for me. This is because it was my first marathon overseas, and also the one that I went below the qualifying time (3:30) for the Boston Marathon in 2007. I finished with the time of 3:19.37. The event had a festival atmosphere with different groups of runners doing varying distances for the day. The route was generally flat and it runs along the coastline, with the sea breeze constantly in your face — it reminded me of our own East Coast Park but the difference was the weather: a cool 10 – 15°C in a sunny setting. The atmosphere along the route was relaxed with supporters along the way cheering the runners on, with the occasional band playing songs for us. One key factor that I will remember was the way the marathon pacers guided us along the way. I ran with the 3:15 pace group and the leader kept us going with simple advice, like taking in fluids at the water stops, being aware of our individual capability — to stay with the pack or move ahead on your own or slow down but not to create unnecessary surges forward to derail the group. I brought back these basic advice and experiences to Singapore, and shared them with fellow runners at the Standard Chartered Singapore Marathon as official pacers for the marathon."

— David Tay, seasoned marathoner and triathlete

Hong Kong Marathon
Hong Kong
February

For those still itching to run after completing the Singapore Marathon, you can head on to the Hong Kong Marathon. The scenic course brings you over majestic bridges stretching across the harbour. With the temperatures in the comfortable teens, overcoming the gentle slopes across the bridges would not be that daunting. The marathon aside, you must not miss the food and shopping that this exciting city has to offer.

"After attending my very first marathon, the Standard Chartered Singapore Marathon, in December 2004, the feeling of crossing the finishing line was so fantastic that I couldn't wait to attend another marathon. So I decide to give Hong Kong Marathon a try just after two months. The race route took me through bustling streets, over three bridges (the magnificent Tsing Ma Bridge has the most beautiful scenery) and

through two tunnels. One of the tunnels is the 2-km Western Harbour Tunnel, which runs underneath the river — the super venturi effect near the exit of the tunnel requires you to make an extra effort to push yourself out of the tunnel. Lastly, you go through a punishing 5 km climb, your muscles threatening to cramp toward the finishing line. The consolation is the nice cool weather in the low 20s, i.e. you feel like you are running in a big air-conditioned room."

— Robson Phan, finisher of the 2005 edition
in a then-personal best time of 3:28:18

Nairobi Marathon
Kenya
October

The Nairobi Marathon is the largest sporting event in Kenya, home of the greatest distance runners in the world. If you want to know what it is like to run in altitude, try out this race. Do not expect to do a personal best, though.

"I have always wondered what it would be like running in Kenya. The opportunities came for me in 2005 and 2008. The course was very hilly and has changed to less steep hills when I returned on my second attempt. The temperature is around 20°C with an average humidity of 55 per cent. There were no distance markers for every kilometre and only plain water was provided at the water points (could hardly find any isotonic drinks in the supermarkets there). At an altitude of between 1,600 to 1,800 m, breathing was slightly laborious but manageable. I would recommend arriving at least two nights before the race and have a easy run to acclimatize to the altitude. Do note that at night there are a lot of mosquitoes, even in the five star hotels! While in Kenya, three of the great things to do are: 1) Go on a Safari, 2) Climb up Kilimanjaro, and 3) Visit a running camp. I stayed and trained in a running camp in Eldoret (a town in western Kenya), the breeding ground for the elite distance running world, where I met Kip Keino and Daniel Komen (current 3,000 m world record holder) and took photos with them!"

— Lua Choon Huat, marathon and ultramarathoner

Xiamen International Marathon
China
January

Touted as "The Most Beautiful Marathon Road on Earth", the whole course, with a 6 hr cut-off time, runs along the scenic seaside town during the cool season on the first Saturday of every January. It has grown in popularity ever since it began in 2003. This course is recommended if you are pursuing a personal best timing, as the course is flat.

"One of my favourite Chinese marathons, with the streets lined up from 0 to 42km with young and older supporters. The cool January weather has helped many qualify for Boston."

— Mohanadas Kandiah, finisher of 71 marathons

**Angkor Wat
International
Half Marathon**
Cambodia
December

What can be more surreal than running amongst Angkor Wat's complex of legendary ancient temples! This race is the perfect excuse to have an exotic holiday in Cambodia. At present, there is no category for the full marathon, but that only gives you fresher legs to do some more sightseeing after the race.

"If you've never visited Cambodia or had the opportunity to visit Angkor Wat, plan your a trip to coincide with this race weekend. It was been one of the most memorable and enjoyable sporting events I've ever participated in. Superbly organised, on a fast, flat, shady, tarmac course. Above all, take time to support local disabled runners and wheelchair participants, for whom this event raises money to help with their rehabilitation following landmine accidents."

— Pauline Mulroy, a die-hard runner who has explored every corner of Asia

APPENDIX 1: 12-WEEK TRAINING LOG

Mesocycle Training Type	Mon	Tue	Wed	Thu	Fri	Sat	Sun	Week Total
Date								1
Target (km)								
Distance (km)								
Time (min)								
Pace (min/km)								
Remarks								
Date								2
Target (km)								
Distance (km)								
Time (min)								
Pace (km/h)								
Remarks								
Date								3
Target (km)								
Distance (km)								
Time (min)								
Pace (min/km)								
Remarks								
Date								4
Target (km)								
Distance (km)								
Time (min)								
Pace (km/h)								
Remarks								
Date								5
Target (km)								
Distance (km)								
Time (min)								
Pace (min/km)								
Remarks								
Date								6
Target (km)								
Distance (km)								
Time (min)								
Pace (km/h)								
Remarks								

								7
Date								
Target (km)								
Distance (km)								
Time (min)								
Pace (min/km)								
Remarks								
Date								8
Target (km)								
Distance (km)								
Time (min)								
Pace (km/h)								
Remarks								
Date								9
Target (km)								
Distance (km)								
Time (min)								
Pace (min/km)								
Remarks								
Date								10
Target (km)								
Distance (km)								
Time (min)								
Pace (km/h)								
Remarks								
Date								11
Target (km)								
Distance (km)								
Time (min)								
Pace (min/km)								
Remarks								
Date								12
Target (km)								
Distance (km)								
Time (min)								
Pace (km/h)								
Remarks								

Run for your Life!
210

APPENDIX 2: *SINGAPORE, MY TRAINING GROUND*

>>*With input from Ben Swee*

As part of your marathon training, you will be running many kilometres. Use this as an opportunity to explore various parts of Singapore — there are many pleasant running routes all over the island. The different routes also allow you to do the whole range of training runs, from base runs, to long slow runs, pace runs, tempo runs, intervals, fartlek, and hill training. The National Parks Board (NParks) has created an extensive park connector network so that you can have long runs with minimal interruptions. Here are some recommended training venues:

Area	Location	Description of Route
East Coast Park	Along East Coast Parkway and East Coast Park Service Road	Singapore's largest and most popular park in the southeast provides a flat route along the beach. It is highly popular with runners and can be crowded on weekends. It is about 10 km from Fort Road to the National Service Resort and Country Club, making it an ideal location for your long slow runs. **Training**: For a 21 km flat course, start at B1 carpark and run eastwards, go past National Sailing Centre, past National Service Resort and Country Club, past NSRCC Sea Sports Centre, and turn around at MOE Changi Coast Adventure Centre to run back to B1 carpark. This is a good route to do your 21 km time trial.
Changi Beach Park/ Changi Coastal Road	Along Nicoll Drive and Changi Coast Road	Changi Beach park is about 3.3 km in length, located in the eastern part of Singapore. With the addition of an 8 km jogging path along the Changi Coast Road towards East Coast Park, it is a pleasant and flat course for your long slow runs. The stretch along the Changi Coast Road does not have any toilets or water fountains, so it is advisable to carry some water with you.
Pasir Ris Park	Pasir Ris Park stretches from Pasir Ris Road to Jalan Loyang Besar and can be accessed through Elias Road and Pasir Ris Green	Stretching about 3 km along the beach, this park presents a flat route and is less crowded compared to East Coast Park. It also offers a great view of the sea, allowing you to feel relaxed and enticing you to have a dip after a run.
Bedok Reservoir Park	Along Bedok Reservoir Road	Quite a number of races are organised here. A single loop around the reservoir is 4.3 km long. Runners can opt to run on gravel or grass, offering an opportunity to train on a different surface. There is not much shade, so it is advisable to run in the early mornings or evenings. **Training**: As there are distance markers, you can do your pace runs, tempo runs, aerobic intervals, and long slow runs here.

Bishan Park	Along Ang Mo Kio Ave 1	Within this beautiful park are ponds and lush greenery lining the jogg ing path, invoking a sense of peacefulness and serenity. Being located minutes from the Bishan MRT station adds to its appeal as an accessible training ground.
Old Upper Thomson Road/ Mandai Road	Adjacent to Upper Thomson Road & Lower Pierce Reservoir Park	With Old Upper Thomson Road located away from the main road, few vehicles ply this road. But do watch out for bicycles and speeding cars. **Training**: For a 21 km moderately hilly run, start at the main car park of MacRitchie Reservoir and run northwards along Upper Thomson Road, then turn left into Old Upper Thomson Road, run past Lower Pierce Reservoir entrance, past Upper Pierce Reservoir entrance, back onto Upper Thomson Road, turn left at Mandai Road, and then turn left into Upper Seletar Reservoir until you reach the public toilet on your left. That would be 10.5 km. Hence a round trip would be a good 21 km run. For a 25 km run, proceed as above, but instead of turning around at the toilet, run past it, following the road until you ascend to the walking path along the Upper Seletar Reservoir. At the end of this elevated path is a large gate. If you turn back at this gate and retrace your way back to MacRitchie, that would be a 25 km, moderately hilly run. For a 34 km run, proceed as above, but instead of turning around at the gate, run past the gate and turn left onto Mandai Road. Continue along Mandai Road and follow the signboards to the Singapore Zoo. Make a u-turn at the car park and retrace your way back to MacRitchie Reservoir main car park. There is a long stretch without toilets between Upper Seletar Reservoir Park and the Singapore Zoo, so do drink up at the beginning and end of that stretch if you are not carrying any water with you.
MacRitchie Reservoir Park	Along Lornie Road	A favourite training area of many, taking runners through the nature trails, forest and boardwalks at the edge of the reservoir and within the park, providing hilly terrain which can take runners anywhere from a few kilometres to more than 10km. With its recent facelift, there are attractive amenities and more parking lots. MacRitchie Runners 25 (MR25), an active running club, organises regular running events here, including 5 km time trials every other month and progressive runs towards the year-end marathon. Every last Sunday of the year, MR25 organizes a 12-hour ultramarathon — it starts at 7 am and you keep running around a 10 km hilly cross-country route to see how many laps you can complete before 7 pm! There are also informal groups that do long runs every Sunday, starting at 7 am — you are welcome to join them. **Training**: Great for cross-country training, with routes of various lengths of up to 10 km. Watch your ankles.

Upper Pierce Reservoir Park	Along Old Upper Thomson Road	This nice reservoir is not as crowded as MacRitchie. You will need a car to get here. **Training**: This is one of the hilliest routes in Singapore. Start at the main car park of the reservoir and run along the road towards the entrance gate and turn left onto Old Upper Thomson Road. Run to the end of Old Upper Thomson Road where it joins onto Upper Thomson Road and make a u-turn back to the car park. This would be about 6 km. Between the car park and gate, there are three rather steep hills. You can do fartlek runs, hilly tempo runs, or intervals up the slopes. Do not try this early on in your training cycles — reserve this location for the occasions when you already have a strong base and wish to push your fitness up a notch.
Fort Canning Park	Bounded by Hill Street, Canning Rise, Clemenceau Avenue and River Valley Road	Located in the heart of the city, this small park has a 2 km route that is peppered with slopes and steps, presenting a challenge to all who train here.
Marina Promenade/ Esplanade Park/Boat Quay/Clark Quay	Along Republic Boulevard/Ave, Connaught Drive, opposite Padang and City Hall, along the Singapore River up to Kim Seng/ Havelock Road	Highly accessible due to its location within the city, it takes runners past various interesting sights along the route such as the Singapore Flyer, Esplanade, watering holes at Boat Quay & Clark Quay, the Singapore River, restaurants, hotels and Singapore's famous night spot, Zouk. Each loop is about 8 km.
Botanic Gardens	1 Cluny Road, via Bukit Timah Road or Holland Road	Just on the outskirts of Orchard, the Botanic Gardens are a favourite with many. The greenery and lakes offer a pleasant distraction from the toil of running. Numerous paths provide a great variety of routes, scenery and distances.
CCA Bukit Timah Track	Evans Road, next to the Jacob Ballas Children's Garden, Singapore Botanic Gardens	This centrally located synthetic track is open to the public and many groups conduct their training here. It gets especially crowded on weekday evenings, so do observe track etiquette by keeping lane 1 clear for runners doing their interval training or time trials. **Training**: The synthetic track is ideal for doing your time trials and interval training. **Training**: Within a short walking distance, Nassim Road and Dalvey Road are ideal for moderately hilly tempo runs or aerobic intervals. Nassim Road measures 1.5 km from Cluny Road to Orchard Road. Dalvey Road stretches 900 m from Cluny Road to Stevens Road.
Bukit Brown Cemetery	At the end of Lorong Halwa. Approach from either Lornie Road or Kheam Hock Road	This quiet cemetery lies on the side of Lornie Road opposite to that of Sime Road. The roads within the cemetery are gently undulating and makes a loop of about 3 km. You will hardly bump into a living soul, so it is a nice place for a peaceful run. It is within jogging distance from the CCA Bukit Timah Track, via Kheam Hock Road, so you can park at the track and jog to the cemetery as warm up. **Training**: Good for gentle hill training. You can do fartlek, base runs, tempo runs, and pace runs here.

Mount Faber Park	Junction of Kampong Bahru Road and Telok Blangah Road, also via Morse Road from West Coast Highway	If a challenge is what you are looking for, this is the ideal training ground. A 1.5 km uphill route from the Kampong Bahru or Morse Road entry will bring you to the top of Mount Faber, where you can have a commanding view of Sentosa island. Within the Park, runners can attempt a 1.6 km Mount Faber Loop, going downhill one way, and uphill the other. **Training**: Popular for advanced hill training.
Labrador Park	Along Labrador Villa Road off Pasir Panjang Road	A small, secluded park on the south coast, where runners can train on the flat path along the water with a panoramic view of the sea, or attempt the short but challenging uphill path to the top.
Kent Ridge Park	Vigilante Drive off South Buona Vista Road. Access via Vigilante Drive, Science Park Drive	Entering Kent Ridge park from the South Buona Vista Road will require runners to overcome a highly challenging steep slope on Vigilante Drive before entering the park with beautiful flora and an excellent view of the southern coastline of Singapore. **Training**: Popular for advanced hill training.
The Southern Ridges	Mount Faber Park, Telok Blangah Hill Park, Kent Ridge Park	Greenery and fantastic views of the city and Southern coast make this hilly 9 km route connecting Mount Faber Park, Telok Blangah Hill Park, Kent Ridge Park, and West Coast Park a popular choice for runners. There are two eye-catching bridges, Henderson Waves and Alexandra Arch, and a canopy walk along the route. **Training**: Great for fartlek or moderate to advanced hill training. You can also do your long slow runs here, but go slow on the slopes.
West Coast Park	Adjacent to West Coast Highway and Clementi Road	A loop of about 4 km takes you through two parts of the park: the first part goes around a huge open space with an adventure playground and a view of the coastline; the second part, located towards the east, is a small forest offering a quiet and peaceful environment.
Sungei Simpang Kiri	Junction between Yishun Ave 2 and Yishun Industrial Park A	This a flat 2.8 km long jogging and cycling path running along Sungei Simpang Kiri, from Yishun Ave 2 to the northern coastline. You've got the canal on your right, lush greenery on your left, and the sea in front of you. There are distance markers every 200 m. **Training**: Running to the end and back covers 5.6 km. The clear distance markers make this track ideal for pace runs, tempo runs, and interval training. If you set your watch to beep every 200 m, you can accurately practice your race pace.
Bukit Batok Nature Park	Bounded by Bukit Batok East Ave 2, Bukit Batok East Ave 6, Lorong Sesuai	The terrain is undulating and footpaths meander through the lush secondary forest leading to look-out points reaching more than 10 storeys high to provide breathtaking views of the former quarry.

APPENDIX 3: *RACE ETIQUETTE*

>>*With input from Tan Peh Khee*

If you are new to road racing, here are a few tips on race etiquette to make the race enjoyable for everyone.

- **Register for the race**. Race organizers need to make provisions (e.g. drinks, food, medical supplies, volunteers, human traffic) for the anticipated number of participants.

- **Stick to your designated corral at the start**. Some races have corrals based on estimated pace — be honest when entering your estimated race time when registering. On race day, start from your designated corral. If there are no corrals, do not crowd the start line ahead of faster runners. There is no need to be at the front as almost all races offer chip time.

- **Do not hold up runners behind you after starting**. Once the gun goes, start running — using handphones, chatting with friends, walking with more than two runners abreast, etc. will hold up the runners behind. This can be dangerous as runners that are forced to cut to the side to overtake runners may get in the way of other runners, compounding the problem. At the start line, the top runners speed off at easily more than 14.0, 14.7, and 15.0 km/h for marathon, half marathon, and 10 km races!

- **Keep to the side**. If you are running with a group of friends, try not to run more than two abreast, otherwise faster runners will not be able to run through smoothly. There is usually a passing lane — keep this lane clear unless overtaking. Be aware of runners behind you who are trying to overtake you — having earphones on does not absolve you from keeping clear.

- **Overtake safely.** When overtaking, especially in crowded conditions where the runner in front may not run in a straight line, warn him or her by calling out, "To your right," if you are overtaking to his or her right and vice versa. Thank runners who make the effort to give way to you.

- **Be considerate to others at the water stations.** Ensure that you are not cutting off other runners while you are grabbing your drink — do not stop abruptly. If you have to slow down to drink, move away from the traffic before doing so. Check your "blind spot" before throwing away the empty paper cups. Aim for the cup collection bins.

- **Show appreciation to volunteers**. Thank or smile at race marshals, first aiders, and other volunteers as you pass them.

- **Acknowledge cheering supporters along the route.** If you are too tired to say "Thanks," a smile, a friendly nod, or thumbs up will suffice.

- **Keep moving after the finish.** There will be runners coming in right behind you, so keep going until it is safe to stop completely.

- **Stay off lane 1 at the track.** When training at the track, do take note that there are many runners doing timed repeats or time trials. If you are simply doing laps without a time target, leave lane 1 (i.e. the innermost lane) clear for these runners to use.

Keep Running!